A Great and Glorious Victory

D1344189

A Great and Glorious Victory

New Perspectives on the Battle of Trafalgar

EDITED BY
RICHARD HARDING

Seaforth
PUBLISHING

A DVD of the Inshore Squadron's animation of the complete battle of Trafalgar
(see Chapter 1) is available separately from the publisher and the 1805 Club.

Copyright © The Nelson Legacy Conference Series Ltd 2008

First published in Great Britain in 2008 by
Seaforth Publishing,
Pen & Sword Books Ltd,
47 Church Street,
Barnsley S70 2AS

British Library Cataloguing in Publication Data
A catalogue record for this book is available from the British Library

ISBN 978 1 84832 008 6

Typeset and designed by JCS Publishing Services Ltd, www.jcs-publishing.co.uk

Printed and bound in Great Britain by Biddles Ltd in King's Lynn, Norfolk

Contents

༄☙☙

Contributors		*vii*
Editor's Acknowledgements		*ix*
Foreword by Admiral Sir Jonathan Band		*xi*
Introduction – The Battle of Trafalgar: New Departures and Positions		1
1	The Reconstruction of Trafalgar	5
2	'Eager and Happy to Exert themselves in forwarding the Public's Service'	30
3	Trafalgar: Myth and History	41
4	Trafalgar: Myth and Reality	58
5	Trafalgar: A French Point of View	70
6	Behind the Wooden Walls: The British Defence against Invasion, 1803–1805	80
7	La Grande Armée of 1805: From the Great Ocean to the Great Continent	90
8	Austerlitz and the French	101
Notes		*113*
Index		*125*

Contributors

꧁⊕꧂

The Inshore Squadron: Dr Alison Barker is a research scientist with a background in plant defences against insect attack. Mark Barker is Designs Approvals Manager for the UK Civil Aviation Authority. Tony Grey has a career in the civil service involving cartography and information management. Malcolm Smalley works in the space industry carrying out mathematical modelling and motion simulation. Together, they have worked on computer-moderated naval wargames for over ten years.

Michael Broers is a Fellow of Lady Margaret Hall, Oxford University, and has been a Visiting Member at the Institute for Advanced Study, Princeton. He is the author of five books, most recently, *The Napoleonic Empire in Italy, 1796–1814: Cultural Imperialism in a European Context?* (2005) which won the Prix Napoléon in 2006.

Michael Duffy is Associate Professor of History at the University of Exeter. He has been Vice President of the Navy Records Society, Director of the Centre for Maritime Historical Studies at Exeter, and Editor of the *Mariner's Mirror*. He is the author of many books and articles on the French Revolutionary and Napoleonic Wars.

Clive Emsley is Professor of History at the Open University. He was educated at the University of York and Peterhouse, Cambridge. He has taught at the University of Paris and held various visiting fellowships at universities in Australia, Canada and New Zealand. His publications include *British Society and the French Wars* (1979) and *Britain and the French Revolution* (2000). His current research focuses on the history of crime and policing in Britain and Europe.

Agustín Guimera is Research Fellow at the Spanish National Research Council (CSIC), Madrid, Spain. His field of interest is the History of the Atlantic systems, of the eighteenth to the twentieth centuries. He has recently studied European naval history in his works *Nelson and Tenerife, 1797* (1999); "Godoy y la Armada", in *Manuel Godoy y su tiempo* (2004); 'Gravina y el liderazgo naval de su tiempo', in *Trafalgar y el mundo atlántico* (2004); "Trafalgar y la marinería española" in *El equilibrio de los imperios. De Utrecht a Trafalgar* (2005); 'Napoleón y la Armada', en *XXXI Congreso Internacional de Historia Militar* (2006). He has coordinated three international conferences on this subject, and is now preparing the edition of the book *Bloqueos navales y operaciones anfibias en las guerras de la Revolución y el Imperio, 1793–1815*.

Richard Harding is Professor of Organisational History at the University of Westminster. He is the author of *Amphibious Warfare in the Eighteenth Century* (1991), *The Evolution of the Sailing Navy* (1995) and *Seapower and Naval Warfare,*

1650–1830 (1999). He has edited a number of books on naval history, and he is a Fellow of the Royal Historical Society and Chairman of the Society for Nautical Research.

Peter Hicks is historian and chargé des affaires internationales at the Fondation Napoléon, Paris, France, and Visiting Research Fellow at the University of Bath, UK. His most recent Napoleonic publications are: an edition of and commentary on Napoleon's novel, *Clisson et Eugénie* (2007), the essay 'The Battle of Austerlitz, Collective Amnesia, and the Non-commemoration of Napoleon in France', in *History, Commemoration, and National Preoccupation: Trafalgar 1805–2005*, ed. Holger Hoock, British Academy Occasional Papers Vol 8, the essay 'Napoleon und sein Hof', in *Napoleon. Trikolore und Kaiseradler über Rhein und Weser*, ed. Veit Veltzke (2007). His current projects include the publication of a little known account of Napoleon on St Helena by the doctor Barry Edward O'Meara. He is currently a member of the Historical Committee for the publication of the complete correspondence of Napoleon I.

Admiral Rémi Monaque is a retired officer of the French Navy. He has written numerous articles on the history of naval thought and on the French navy of the eighteenth century. His publications include a biography of Admiral Latouche-Tréville (2000) and *Trafalgar, 21 Octobre 1805* (2005).

Dr Colin White is currently Director of the Royal Naval Museum in the Historic Dockyard in Portsmouth. He has published widely on Nelson and the Navy of his time and has made a particular study of Nelson's letters and of his leadership style and the development of his tactical thought. As Director of the Nelson Letters Project from 2000 to 2006, he was responsible for locating some 1,500 hitherto unpublished Nelson letters, in archives all over the world. His subsequent book, *Nelson: The New Letters* (2005) won the Distinguished Book Award from the Society for Military History. His latest book is *Nelson the Admiral* (2005), a detailed study of Nelson's professional career, based on all the new material. He is Visiting Professor of Naval History at the University of Portsmouth.

Editor's Acknowledgements

THIS SMALL COLLECTION OF essays is presented as a starting point for future research. I am grateful to the authors for their co-operation in putting this volume together. I am also grateful to Mr Peter Warwick of the 1805 Club and Dr Nick Slope of the Nelson Society for their advice and support, and Mr Julian Thomas of the Royal Naval Museum, Portsmouth. Without the support of the Museum and the Society for Nautical Research, there would have been no bicentenary conference (which was held at the Royal Naval Museum, Portsmouth, between 13 and 15 October 2005) and consequently no papers to edit. The assistance of Mr Julian Mannering of Seaforth Publishing has been invaluable in bringing this work to fruition. Finally, I am very grateful to the First Sea Lord, Sir Jonathan Band, for his preface. Not only was Sir Jonathan an important contributor to the original conference, but he has been extremely supportive of the role that history has to play in informing the modern navy and contemporary society of the maritime dimension of life. In the light of the success of the bicentenary conference, a new conference series, the Nelson Legacy Conference Series, has been initiated and already held its first conference, with the purpose of taking the study forward. In 2005 scholars of many nations proved that although Trafalgar is like many iconic battles, it is also different. It does not have to be immured in a national myth. A critical re-evaluation using new methods or employing new perspectives can take an event at sea two hundred years ago and demonstrate to a contemporary audience that it is relevant to our understanding of wider historical issues and our present-day concerns. A CD-ROM of the Inshore Squadron's presentation is available separately from the publishers and the 1805 Club. Please visit www.1805Club.org for details.

Foreword

THE BICENTENARY COMMEMORATION OF the Battle of Trafalgar provided a timely reminder of the vital role of the sea in Britain's national history. However, the research that it stimulated, from scholars of many nations, demonstrated that understanding the battle offered much more to those willing to look. The themes that emerged have broader lessons. By painstakingly detailed attention to sources, historians have reinforced many important factors that make the difference between success and failure. Stripped of national myths, the Battle of Trafalgar confirms some important truths. Careful planning, shared understanding, flexibility in application, co-operation and mutual support and the importance of leadership that builds morale and promotes initiative were all vital to the outcome of that battle. These issues are clearly reflected in this collection of essays. What these studies of Trafalgar also show is that while there are many points of agreement on impact or consequences, perceptions of dramatic events are conditioned by the local environment. Contributions to this collection indicate that as European nations are closer now, so there is evidence of a shared understanding of a shared past. Nevertheless, they also show that understanding the differences of perceptions is just as important.

The conference that generated these papers was a fitting climax to a year of commemoration. It proves that commemoration, informed by solid historical research, is a starting point for fresh thinking, not just about specific events, like the battle off Cape Trafalgar two hundred years ago, but the way we understand our relationship with the sea, our neighbours and maritime power.

Admiral Sir Jonathon Band KCB ADC
First Sea Lord and Chief of Naval Staff

The Battle of Trafalgar

New Departures and Positions

RICHARD HARDING

B ATTLES AND WARS PLAY a central part in national myths. Victories, real or imagined, are events that provide a focus for the narratives of national creation, survival or unity. It is not surprising that the events of the wars or battles are quickly overlaid with interpretations and even fictions that serve the national story more than they explain the fighting and suffering of the time. In this respect the Battle of Trafalgar on 21 October 1805 is not unusual. It has an iconic status, along with the defeat of the Spanish Armada in 1588 and the Battle of Britain in 1940, as a battle that preserved national independence and demonstrated the particular capabilities and courage of the armed services and people of the nation. Also like other iconic battles, historians have, over decades, and generally outside the public perception of the battle, developed a more sophisticated, nuanced and ambiguous story of the event. Seldom do these interpretations ruffle the public's vision of the heroic and decisive clash of arms.

In one respect, however, Trafalgar is different. In 2005 the bicentenary caught the imagination of the public and media, and for a short period the battle attracted attention far beyond anything previously experienced. The reasons for this are a subject worthy of serious study in themselves. The general orthodoxy is that the British public is not particularly sea-minded. Even less so are they engaged with sailing battle fleets and old quarrels with France and Spain. If the British were not expected to be concerned about Trafalgar, then it could be expected that this was even truer of the rest of the world, particularly France and Spain.

For whatever reasons, the battle attracted immense attention and gave a rare space for more varied and complex aspects of the battle to be presented. The public in general may have forgotten the variety of new interpretations that were printed in newspapers and broadcast in documentaries, and may now have settled back with their traditional view of Trafalgar (another important subject for study), but those interested in naval history have been left with a rich legacy. Particularly, there are many new biographies, not just of Nelson, but of other officers on both sides, to inform our thinking of the battle and early nineteenth-century navies in general. The battle – as a tactical and strategic event, from the British, French and Spanish perspectives – has naturally attracted renewed attention. The cultural impact of the battle on the nineteenth and twentieth centuries was a relatively new area of study, which may not have been so fully explored without the stimulus of the bicentenary.[1]

Between 13 and 15 October 2005, a conference was assembled at the Royal Naval Museum, Portsmouth to examine the battle. In some respects it was an attempt to consolidate so much activity and scholarship that had been published or broadcast over the previous twelve months, but in others it was an attempt to broaden out and suggest new areas for study. This selection of papers has been collated with the idea that the legacy of the bicentenary should not just be seen as the culmination of research and scholarship, but a stepping-off point for further investigation.

The centre-piece of the conference was a presentation of the battle by the Inshore Squadron, a group of naval historians and wargamers who use computer technology in their interest. The wargame has had an important role to play in military history since the mid-nineteenth century, but the availability of relational databases, which can record the impact of changes in individual variables (in this case, observations from masters' logs) across a large data set has great potential in the analysis of naval battles. The Inshore Squadron had used this technique to examine the battles of the Nile (1798) and Copenhagen (1801), but this was their most ambitious project yet – sixty major warships, with both fleets in motion. The value of the tool still relies on the traditional skills of the historian – meticulous examination and understanding of primary data. It relies on the historian's judgement as to the weight to give to each piece of evidence, but once those decisions are made, the technology allows us to appreciate how an individual piece of evidence may alter our perception of the battle space as a whole. The essay printed here is both an explanation of the battle as the members of the Inshore Squadron recreated it, and some of the conclusions about the battle that they were able to draw from it. Continual testing, refinement and application to other battles, holds out the promise of new steps forward in the study of the tactical aspects of naval battles.

Tactical aspects of Trafalgar received great attention during the bicentenary and the essays here reflect some of the most important issues that have emerged. Perhaps the most pervasive issue, which remains at the very centre for students of the battle, is the role of Nelson himself. What did he contribute to the battle? He was mortally wounded within two hours of the commencement of the battle, yet no historian could exclude him from consideration. Professors White and Duffy, Dr Guimera and Admiral Monaque agree that while the infrastructure of the Royal Navy – its material, its training and traditions – were far better than their enemies, it was not universally effective. The Royal Navy required leadership to make it the powerful force that it was. Professor Colin White is in an excellent position to analyse Nelson as an admiral. Nelson's leadership over the weeks before the battle was fundamental to his success on the day. His leadership of the men and his attitude to command allowed him flexibility of manoeuvre and confidence that very few other commanders would have had in the same circumstances. The 'Nelson Touch', which became a legend after the battle, is given clearer definition and is now capable of further analysis in the context of nineteenth- and twentieth-century naval command. Professor

Michael Duffy and Admiral Monaque show how Nelson's command situation contrasted dramatically with that of his opponents, Admirals Villeneuve and Gravina. However, Dr Guimera points out that Franco-Spanish command was not as poor as is often asserted. The points that divide these scholars show that there is still plenty of scope for further study. The role of leadership emerges powerfully from these essays, as it has in others, and suggests important new areas for research.

Beyond the battle and campaign at sea, there is the question of its impact on the diplomatic and strategic environment. It is commonly understood today that by the time Trafalgar was fought, Napoleon's threat to invade Britain was over for the time being. Napoleon had already marched his army from the Channel coast to the Danube. Dr Michael Broers' examination of Napoleon's response to the enforced inactivity at Boulogne camp, 1803–5, shows that the Emperor had not wasted his time. Internal reforms in France, a refocusing of diplomatic priorities and the training and development of the Grande Armée were the foundations of the new Napoleonic Empire about to be carved out as a result of Austerlitz, Jena and Friedland. The diplomatic consequences of this are also considered by Dr Peter Hicks. Possibly far more important – in the immediate term – than the battle of Trafalgar, was Britain's success in bringing Austria into the anti-French coalition. This shifted (irreversibly, as it turned out) the strategic centre of gravity in the great European struggle from the Channel to Central Europe. Was it Britain's diplomatic triumph with Austria, combined with Napoleon's organisational successes and subsequent diplomatic responses over the summer of 1805, rather than the Battle of Trafalgar, that shaped the future of Napoleonic foreign policy and ultimately over-extended the Empire? In this context, Trafalgar was, from the French point of view, a tragic waste, irrelevant to the main struggle.

The British viewed it rather differently. Trafalgar was not irrelevant, but neither was it utterly decisive. Professor Clive Emsley's study of the land forces raised to resist invasion shows how, despite Trafalgar, the threat of invasion was taken seriously long after 1805, leading to an impressive mobilisation of manpower. If Napoleon's army had remained at Boulogne and Trafalgar had been lost, it would not have opened the way to immediate invasion, for Sir William Cornwallis' squadron still stood in the Western Approaches. Although it was unlikely that the militia and volunteers would have stood up to the well-drilled regiments of the Grande Armée, the sheer scale of British mobilisation and the attrition of the sea crossing made an invasion a highly speculative venture. Nonetheless, as the Napoleonic Empire consolidated in Europe between 1805 and 1807, there was no guarantee that the French troops would not re-assemble one day on the Channel coast.

Looking back on the war, hindsight and contemporary concerns made it possible for judgements to be different. Drs Broers and Hicks both point to the roles Trafalgar and Austerlitz played in the creations of the British and French national myths. The supposed virtues attached to the individualism of free maritime commerce or a Roman heritage carry with them assumptions about why campaigns and battles were fought and won. They also inform the presumed consequences of those victories. It is clear that although the revolutionary and Napoleonic Wars at land and sea have been studied in great detail for over one hundred years, there are still questions about how events at sea influenced war and diplomacy ashore. The bicentenary has done something to give these questions greater focus, if not provide the answers.

Richard Harding

– 1 –

The Reconstruction of Trafalgar

THE INSHORE SQUADRON (MARK BARKER, ALISON BARKER, TONY GRAY, MALCOLM SMALLEY)

✦✦✦

> The Battle of Trafalgar has been so thoroughly threshed out by historians that little new light is thrown on the incidents of the action by the narratives contained in the log books.
>
> T Sturges Jackson, *Logs of the Great Sea Fights* (1900)[1]

W RITTEN OVER A CENTURY ago, this statement admirably describes the Inshore Squadron's main concern in preparing for the Trafalgar Conference. After two hundred years, what could possibly remain unsaid about this iconic battle?

The Traditional View – Commencement of the Battle of Trafalgar

The traditional view of Trafalgar has become part of the national consciousness. The British fleet, formed into two lines, sails directly for the combined Franco-Spanish line under a barrage of fire before breaking the line at right angles and overwhelming the Combined Fleet with devastating close-range broadsides. A simple case of getting into action as quickly as possible, Nelson's attack seems devoid of tactical interest. As with our previous reconstructions of the battles of the Nile and Copenhagen, preparations for Trafalgar began with a review of as many previously published accounts of the battle as could be obtained. Once again, it was found that successive historians placed great reliance on their predecessor's works, in this case particularly the works of James[2] in 1837 and Taylor[3] in 1950, to the extent that inconsistencies in those versions have been faithfully repeated and accepted as received wisdom.

Even the recollections of those actually present need to be treated with care. As well as the natural confusion caused by the chaos of battle, several accounts were written many years after the battle and some writers seem to have checked their memories with the published accounts (particularly James) to confirm the identities of their opponents. In common with their British counterparts, French and Spanish accounts sometimes exaggerate the part played by an individual ship, but were essential in confirming ship positions and identities.

We concluded that reliance had to be placed upon contemporary material and eye-witness accounts as recorded in logs and journals, comparing the sequence and timings of these records by drawing up a coordinated timeline of key events. Each ship's course during the battle was mapped out and a running plot created using a computer simulation.

It quickly became apparent that the traditional version of Trafalgar was far too simplistic. How could *Victory*'s mizzen be shot away if she was approaching the Combined Fleet at right angles to the line? Why did her Master's Log[4] clearly report passing 'down the enemy line'? What was the explanation for the forty-five minute difference between *Royal Sovereign* and *Victory* breaking the line? And how did the actual attack compare with Nelson's famous Memorandum and the dramatic sketch of his intentions discovered by Colin White[5] during the Nelson's Letters project?

In the run-up to the first centenary celebrations the wisdom of Nelson's apparent headlong rush into battle generated such controversy that an Admiralty Committee was appointed to report on the tactics used at Trafalgar. As part of the preparations for the Bridge Report published in 1913,[6] we found that Captain TH Tizard of the Royal Navy had collated the details of the approach phase of the British ships in a manner reminiscent of our own researches.

The work of the Bridge Report finished with a diagram of the battle at noon on the 21 October 1805. For the Bicentenary Conference, the Inshore Squadron determined to resolve the questions we had raised and produce a twenty-first-century follow-on to the Bridge Report from noon until the end of the battle. Using the advantages of modern technology, the course and actions of each individual ship during the battle were reconstructed using a computer simulation and the resulting animation presented to the conference, together with a scale model showing the height of the battle at 13.00.

06.00–12.00: The Approach

When dawn broke shortly before 06.00 on the morning of 21 October 1805, Horatio Nelson looked on the culmination of two years of planning and implacable pursuit. Silhouetted by the rising sun around ten miles to the north-east lay the Combined Fleet, a total of thirty-three ships formed into three squadrons and sailing south-south-east towards the Straits of Gibraltar and the Mediterranean.

Nelson's own force of twenty-seven vessels was in night-cruising formation, with only *Africa* out of position – having missed an instruction to wear during the night – now well off to the North. At 06.10 he issued the order to Form the Order of Sailing in Two Columns, followed by the order to Bear Up and Sail Large (the fastest point of sailing) to the east-north-east.

At 06.22 Nelson gave the order to Prepare for Battle, followed twenty minutes later by a course change to steer directly to the east. The fresh breezes and squalls of the previous night had now died away, and even with every sail set it would take at least five hours to cross the intervening distance.

On board *Bucentaure*, Villeneuve watched as the British fleet deployed into two loose lines, described by onlookers as *peletons*. Today this term is most commonly used to describe the main pack of cyclists in the Tour de France, and this gives a good impression of the irregular linear formations that formed, unhindered by any pre-determined order of battle. Nelson's instruction for the order of sailing as per order of battle was already having the desired effect of saving precious time during the deployment.

As soon as it became apparent that the British main body was present, as well as the shadowing frigates, Villeneuve knew that battle was inevitable. At around 06.20 he issued the order to form Line of Battle on the Starboard tack, with himself in the *Bucentaure* in the centre division, Dumanoir in the *Formidable* commanding the rear and Alava in the *Santa Ana* the van, accompanied by Gravina's Squadron of Observation commanded from the *Príncipe de Asturias*.

Villeneuve's tactical options were limited – by the weather, the position of the British fleet and, as he well knew, by the levels of training in the varied fleet he had under his command. Any attempt to escape into the Atlantic would only hasten their interception, given the direction of the wind – the British were holding the windward position. The decreasing south-westerly winds were also accompanied by an ominous heavy swell, a sure sign of an approaching storm pressing the waters ahead of it into rolling undulations several metres high.[7]

An easterly course into the Mediterranean also presented problems. Villeneuve knew that Nelson had detached a strong squadron of six ships towards Gibraltar, indeed, its departure was one of his reasons for sailing. To Villeneuve, Nelson's course showed an intention to concentrate on the rear and cut the Combined Fleet off from the refuge of Cádiz. He had already seen the results of Nelson overwhelming one end of a fleet while the remainder lay paralysed at the Nile, and had predicted such a move in his own tactical instructions. After a long period of deliberation, Villeneuve ordered the fleet to reverse course and wear around, keeping Cádiz to leeward – a potential retreat from storm or battle damage.

Given the lightness of the winds and the effect of the swell, such a manoeuvre would have tested any fleet used to operating together and in regular order. The Combined Fleet was neither of these, and the manoeuvre took almost two hours to perform, each ship struggling to get around and trying to reach its allotted place in the reformed line. Many ships never found their intended station and slotted in where they could.

In the reversed formation Dumanoir now commanded the van, steering a course as close to the wind as possible, followed by Villeneuve in the centre. To the rear, Alava in the *Santa Ana* pressed on to try to close up to the centre, being increasingly forced out to leeward. Gravina's Squadron of Observation, although intended to remain to windward to form a mobile reserve and intercede where needed, steered into the wake of Alava's division to form a continuous line. This resulted in the familiar crescent, sometimes two or three ships deep and with the van steering generally to the north-north-west.

Writing after the battle, Collingwood considered that this formation could have been a deliberate counter to ships breaking the line, as British ships passing through were often faced with further ships firing at them, but the truth is that this was accident rather than intention. Overlapping had the effect of substantially reducing the defensive firepower of a line of battle, and many ships were unable to fire at the British during the approach as they did not have a clear field of fire.

Once the haze of the day was replaced by enveloping clouds of powder smoke, blown back into the faces of the Combined Fleet by the feeble breeze, long-range gunnery became increasingly impractical.

The lightness of the wind was also a concern to Nelson, as this increased the time that his ships would be in danger from enemy fire before reaching the line. To minimise this risk, the lead ships went into action with virtually every sail set, including the unwieldy studding sails on their extended booms. Even so, with the ships managing a maximum of two knots, each would be vulnerable to incoming fire for around fifteen minutes as it crossed the thousand-yard effective range of the opposing guns.

It is popularly supposed that French and Spanish gunners preferred firing high to disable the rigging, but there is no documentary evidence of any such doctrine. The leeward position, with the broadside facing into the wind, tended to make fire go high, as did a lack of experience at the guns. There was also a technological difference, as all of the British guns were fitted with purpose-built flintlocks that allowed firing at a particular instant in the ship's roll. These were by no means standard in the Combined Fleet – an improvised solution using musket locks was in use on at least some.

Records of gunnery exercises between *Formidable* and *Bucentaure* in 1804[8] showed that the best-manned ships of the Combined Fleet could achieve rates of fire comparable with those of the Royal Navy, yet the fact remains that not a single British ship was prevented from reaching the line by rigging damage during the approach. Lying broadside-on to the swell, and making scarcely enough progress to maintain steerage way, the gunners of the Combined Fleet had to cope with an undulating motion which made accurate sighting for elevation, and therefore range, practically impossible. As a result, the British squadrons were able to close the distance in the face of hundreds of guns without suffering crippling damage – the majority of shot either flew too high or ploughed into the sea. As the range diminished however, the situation would become more even.

Trafalgar is unique in that it is the only battle at which Nelson was in overall command where both sides were in motion. It is possible to show both the Nile and Copenhagen using static diagrams, as the opposition were at anchor, but Trafalgar does not lend itself to this approach as the ships of the Combined Fleet travelled over three miles between the time taken for the first and last ships in the British squadrons to engage. The creation of a computer animation allowed an understanding of the development of the battle and the relationship between the separate actions fought by Collingwood and Nelson (Figure 1).

The most comprehensive study of the formation of the Combined Fleet was undertaken by Edouard Desbrière in 1907,[9] the results of which were adopted by the Bridge Committee without revision. The 1933 English translation of this study, now one of the rarest of the Trafalgar volumes and never reprinted, gives a justification for the initial positions of the ships based on log entries and reports of the battle from French and Spanish participants.

This analysis was reviewed and cross-checked with Edward Fraser's 1907 *The Enemy at Trafalgar*[10] and the British logs and journals, and provided sufficient evidence to indicate that the relative positions given by Desbrire, and included

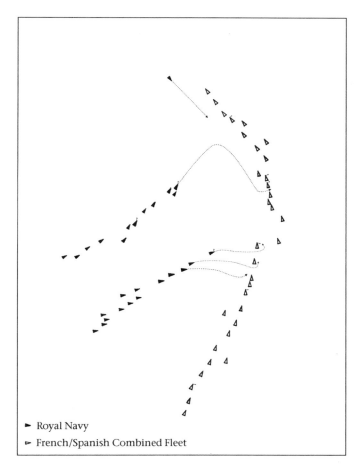

Figure 1: Opening position, 12.00

in the Bridge Report, were largely accurate, with the exception of the spacing between the ships. As will be seen, many British ships encountered difficulties in breaking through the line due to the closeness of the ships of the Combined Fleet, yet the diagram in the Bridge Report shows gaps of up to several hundred yards between succeeding ships.

These positions differ in important details from those given in James, which contains errors that have been repeated in many succeeding accounts. James took his identification of the rear of the Combined Fleet from a widely published diagram drawn up by Magendie, Villeneuve's Captain of the Fleet, which unfortunately reversed the order of the Squadron of Observation. This had the erroneous effect of moving the *San Juan Nepomuceno* from the rearmost ship of the fleet to the heart of James's account of the action, around the *Belleisle* and *Bellerophon* – an error repeated in many subsequent accounts.

On the British side, Captain Tizard's analysis of the positions from comparing log and journal entries was plotted, and again generally confirmed the relative positioning, except in the matter of spacing. Having established the sequence, and timings as to when each ship engaged, in our timeline, in several cases the suggested gaps between ships were so large that they could never have got into action. In these cases, the opening positions were recalculated given the known speeds to ensure that it was possible to reach the line at the appropriate time.

In the case of the *Revenge*, Tizard had to suggest two alternate positions, and he was unable to firmly establish a position for *Africa, Agamemnon, Defence, Defiance* and *Thunderer*. For the latter three ships, accounts unavailable to Tizard[11] have since been published, and these have enabled some of the blanks to be filled in. Where no firm data exists, positions were calculated that would allow each ship to reach any point of the battle where its presence was noted by other vessels. This iterative process required many revisions of the opening position before a version was achieved that was consistent with all of the subsequent evidence.

12.00–13.00: Collingwood's Squadron

A key feature of the Trafalgar Memorandum was the extent to which Nelson delegated control of the leeward attack to Collingwood: 'The Second in Command will have the entire direction of his line to make the attack upon the Enemy.'

Aside from two mischievous signals (09.49, 10.10) for *Mars* to take the lead of the leeward division (an order that Collingwood, with every sail set, had no intention of permitting to succeed), Nelson kept to this arrangement throughout the approach.

As soon as he arrived on station, Nelson had ensured that Collingwood had a ship equal to his task, ordering him to transfer his flag from the slow ninety-eight- gun *Dreadnought* to the hundred-gun *Royal Sovereign*. Freshly re-coppered at Plymouth Dockyard, the 'West Country Waggon' would belie her own reputation for poor sailing by drawing ahead of the rest of the division to become the first ship in range of the guns of the Combined Fleet.

Astern of the *Royal Sovereign* followed the *Belleisle* (74) and *Mars* (74), at first glance both third-rates of the type that formed the backbone of the British Fleet. However, this description does not reflect the firepower that Collingwood had at the head of his division.

Belleisle was a captured French vessel and substantially larger than the standard types of British 74. Both she and *Mars* carried 24-pdrs on their upper gun decks as opposed to the 18-pdrs of the more numerous Common or Middling 74s and were additionally fitted with fearsome batteries of 32-pdr carronades on their top-decks. *Belleisle* was in fact the most heavily armed third-rate in the Royal Navy, and inside effective carronade range (five hundred yards or less) fired a weight of broadside more normally associated with a three-decker first-rate.

It is a feature of the French and Spanish accounts that British three-deckers appear everywhere during the battle, and, although it makes for a better account to be attacked by a three-decker, the presence of heavy-calibre carronades on the topsides may well have contributed to an impression of being fired on by three full gun-decks.

As well as carronades, the British fleet possessed another more subtle technological advantage, in that their gunpowder was more effective. The introduction of an industrial process to manufacture charcoal in iron cylinders had produced gunpowder of much greater power, so much so that it had to be blended with normal powder to avoid overstressing the guns. Even this mix was found to be 15 per cent more powerful than captured French powder, compensating for the heavier guns of the Combined Fleet.[12]

Early on during the approach Collingwood directed his own form of attack by ordering the formation of a line of bearing to the south-west. Also known as a bow-and-quarter line, with each ship maintaining station with a ship off its bow and another off the opposite stern quarter, Collingwood's squadron would approach the rear arc of the Combined Fleet on a broad front, rather than in line ahead. There were several advantages to this method, the theory of which dated back to Anson and Hawke,[13] with each ship in the rear of the Combined Fleet being attacked more quickly, and no delay introduced by needing to accommodate the widely different sailing rates of the British ships. Although each ship should have theoretically adjusted sail to maintain station on its fellows and keep the diagonal line of bearing, this did not happen in practice – among several others, Captain Codrington of the *Orion* remarking 'We all scrambled into battle as soon as we could.'[14]

Nelson's Memorandum called for Collingwood to cut the line twelve ships from the rear, but by 12.00 Collingwood was steering for a gap between Alava's flagship, the 112-gun *Santa Ana*, and the following 74-gun ship, *Fougeux*. It is not clear whether Collingwood was unable to see some of the rearmost ships of the Combined Fleet to leeward and miscounted, or whether he decided that a three-decker flagship was a natural opponent, but the decision meant that he in fact cut the line sixteen ships ahead of the rear – some ships of his division were heavily outnumbered for a time before support arrived. There is no doubt, however, that his action prevented several fresh ships from the rear of the Combined Fleet from threatening Nelson's hard-pressed ships in the centre, later in the battle.

At 12.00 *Fougeux* opened fire on the approaching *Royal Sovereign*, joined shortly afterward by *Santa Ana* and from extreme distance by *Indomptable, San Justo, Neptune* and *San Leandro*. *Fougeux* made sail to attempt to close up the gap to *Santa Ana* and prevent the *Royal Sovereign* from breaking through, but as the distance narrowed she saw that the three-decker would be able to rake her across the bows without reply, and so sheered away to starboard. As she did so, *Royal Sovereign* returned fire with her starboard guns.

Forging ahead, Collingwood took the *Royal Sovereign* close under the *Santa Ana*'s stern and at 12.15 poured in a tremendous raking broadside before turning to port and engaging from leeward. At this range the swell made no difference, and far from being crippled by the attack, *Santa Ana*'s return broadside heeled the *Royal Sovereign* over by several plank widths as it crashed into the British ship's topsides. The two flagships then moved slowly to the north, fighting yardarm-to-yardarm. For the first ten minutes or so, *Royal Sovereign* was the only British ship to have reached the line of the Combined Fleet and was being fired on at differing distances by six enemy ships. As Collingwood later remarked, 'I thought it a long time after I got through their line before I found my friends around me.'[15]

Support was at hand, however, and at around 12.25 *Belleisle* reached the line astern of *Fougeux*, who had continued her turn to starboard to bring her guns to bear with *Indomptable*, adding her fire from leeward. Engaged by a succession of ships over the next three hours, *Belleisle* would become the only British ship to be completely dismasted. The sequence of events around *Belleisle* during this period is critical to understanding the entire southern half of the battle, and we have included a detailed rehearsal of the evidence in the relevant part of this chapter (see pp 21–3).

Belleisle was by no means alone in being hard-pressed – as *Mars* approached at around 12.30 she found her way barred by Cosmao-Kerjulian's *Pluton* and was unable to break through, instead turning to port to engage from windward. The two ships continued to the north firing at point-blank range. Shortly afterwards *Tonnant* broke the line ahead of *Algésiras* and ran foul of her, while the *Bellerophon* got through astern of *Bahama* and collided with *Aigle*. Soon afterwards, she found herself being engaged by three other ships as well: *Monarca* on her port bow, *Bahama* on the port quarter and the French *Swiftsure*, who had needed to bear up to avoid colliding with *Aigle*, from astern.

Relief arrived in the shape of the *Colossus*, who now broke the line astern of the French *Swiftsure*, engaging that ship and the *Bahama* to port. The French *Argonaute* now emerged through the smoke from starboard and also engaged *Colossus*. As a result of over ninety minutes close action fought against these three ships, it was in fact *Colossus* that would suffer the heaviest casualties of all of the British ships that day. By 12.45 the *Revenge*, one of the fastest sailing ships in the fleet, had reached the line to pass astern of *San Ildefonso*, barely avoiding a full collision with the French *Achille*, which had moved ahead to close up the gap.

By now half of Collingwood's division was in close action, while to the north, Nelson had just reached the line in *Victory*. Over the next hour, the remainder of the division engaged the rear of the Combined Fleet in succession. *Defiance* was unable to break the line astern of Gravina's flagship *Príncipe de Asturias* and also had to fight from windward, while the British *Achille* engaged the Spanish *Argonauta*. *Thunderer* bore up to attack the *Berwick*, while the French *Achille* now wore under the stern of the *Revenge*, who had started to move up the leeward side of the line. As Nelson had predicted in his Memorandum – 'Some ships may not get through their exact place, but they will always be at hand to assist their friends and if any are thrown around the rear of the Enemy they will effectively compleat the business of Twelve Sail of the Enemy.'

As we have seen, Collingwood's division was in fact now engaging sixteen ships, and the final group of British ships, comprising *Dreadnought*, *Swiftsure*, *Polyphemus* and *Defence*, did indeed wear around the end of the Combined Fleet and move up to support on the leeward side. Eventually the benefits of mutual support and individual ship-to-ship superiority in gunnery would tell in favour of the British, but the Trafalgar myth of a rapid victory once the line of the Combined Fleet was broken bears little resemblance to the reality of the battle as experienced by Collingwood's ships.

12.00–12.30: Nelson's Squadron

When the first broadsides of the Combined Fleet erupted to the south as the *Royal Sovereign* neared the line, Nelson's lead ships were still three-quarters of a mile away from closing the gap to the enemy. Earlier in the day, Nelson had made provision for those ships he expected to have difficulty keeping up with the approach, signalling for the *Britannia, Prince* and *Dreadnought*, all notoriously slow sailors, to 'take station as convenient without regard to the established order of sailing'.

Africa, separated to the north as a result of missing one of the signals to wear during the previous night, was also instructed to make more sail. Although probably intended to get the *Africa* out of harm's way and allow her to rejoin, this was taken by her captain, Digby, as an instruction to get into action as soon as possible, so the 64-gun ship raced south, exchanging distant broadsides with the whole of the French van as she went.

Leading the windward line was the 100-gun *Victory*. Already 40 years old, she had been thoroughly refitted in 1803. Although not as heavily armed as some of the other first-rates, carrying no carronades other than the famous pair of 68-pdr 'smashers', *Victory* had a reputation for fast sailing that made her a popular choice of flagship. Forever associated with Trafalgar, the 68-pdr was in fact a very uncommon weapon, as the shot was extremely heavy to handle in action, and when *Victory* was repaired after the battle she was rearmed with the more common 32-pdr carronades.

Following close astern to starboard – so close in fact that Nelson had to instruct her captain to keep proper station 'astern of *Victory*' – came *Temeraire*, a virtually new 98-gun ship with a full battery of fourteen 32-pdr carronades on her top-decks. Slightly further back and off to port was *Neptune*, another 98 which, accordingly to Midshipman Badcock 'took it into her head to sail better that morning than I ever remember to have seen her do before'.[16]

These three ships sailed somewhat ahead of the rest of the line, forming a tremendously powerful arrowhead of ships under a full press of sail. One of the common features that can be seen during the development of Nelson's plans is the concentration of heavy ships at the head of the line to provide impetus to the attack. This was not a new concept, but in fact dates from the writing of the French tactician, Viscomte de Morogue in 1763: 'At sea the gun decides the fate of battles. The advantage should be with him who knows how to mass the most firepower in a given place.'[17] While the famed Admiral Suffren was known to favour this approach, and Rodney actually added two articles to the Fighting Instructions to this effect, neither managed to carry it out in battle. The first time the concept was actually delivered in a fleet action was under Nelson's command at Trafalgar.

The remainder of Nelson's division stayed in a loose line ahead, with the 74-gun *Leviathan* and *Conqueror* preceding the 100-gun *Britannia*, flagship of the third-in-command, Lord Northesk. *Britannia* was the oldest first-rate present and a heavy sailor, and may well have been the last ship to carry the heavy 42-pdr guns into battle. In all other cases these had been replaced with the lighter 32-pdr which was easier to handle in action and could be fired more quickly with little loss of hitting power.

So how did Nelson intend to deploy his division in the attack? The Trafalgar Memorandum clearly indicates Nelson's original intention to attack in three divisions, and this intent was graphically confirmed with Colin White's discovery of a contemporary sketch in Nelson's own hand. This also shows three divisions, the van keeping the front portion of the Combined Fleet out of action, while the centre and rear divisions cut the line to create a situation of local superiority for the British fleet.

As Nelson explained to Captain Keats at the garden at Merton, the van squadron would consist of fast two-deckers commanded by 'a trusted officer' – in this case probably Rear Admiral Louis. A succession of orders of battle and sailing from 1803 to 1805 show Nelson's meticulous planning and the development of his tactical thoughts during this period, but as soon as Nelson signalled for the attack in two columns, he was deviating from the plan of attack detailed in the Memorandum – why?

The answer is that, just as at the Nile and Copenhagen, Nelson had to improvise and adapt to the prevailing circumstances. When he wrote the Memorandum he was counting on having forty ships, whereas he now had twenty-seven, with Louis detached to Gibraltar for supplies essential to remain on station. With insufficient ships to follow his original plan, he took on the role of the third squadron with his own division, and at 11.00 ordered a change of course of a point to port, recorded in the log of the *Orion*.

However, the evidence from the Memorandum shows that this method of attack was no casual impulse – there is a handwritten notation on some copies: 'Blue Flag with Yellow Fly – Cut through the enemy's line and engage them on the other side. NB . . . The Admiral will probably advance his fleet to the van of theirs before he makes the signal in order to deceive the Enemy by inducing them to suppose it is his intention to attack their van.'[18] A more succinct summary of the path that Nelson's division would follow is hard to imagine.

The majority of plans of Trafalgar at 12.00 show *Victory* pointing directly at the *Santísima Trinidad* and *Bucentaure* in the centre, but there is no doubt that Nelson's attack at this point was aimed directly towards Dumanoir's van squadron. Compelling evidence for this comes from the log of *Victory*'s own sailing master: 'At 4 minutes past 12, opened our fire on the enemy's van in passing down their line' and is confirmed by the logs of Dumanoir's squadron, such as *Scipion*: 'one of the three-deckers leading the Northern column, which was standing for the centre of our van'[19] and the ships closer to Villeneuve in the centre, such as *San Augustin*: 'One of the columns steered for the centre of the van and thence, hauling to the wind, towards the centre.'[20]

There is even a contemporary visual record – the most commonly published version of Magendie's diagram shows two clean lines of British ships piercing the Combined Fleet at right angles and may well have helped to establish the

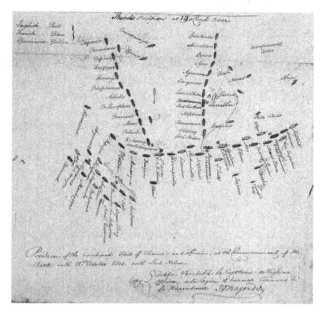

Positions of the Combined Fleets of France and Spain at the commencement of the Battle of 21 October with Lord Nelson. Anonymous pen and ink sketch, copied from Captain Magendie's original drawn aboard the Neptune *and dated 28 October 1805. (National Maritime Museum, Greenwich, London.)*

'traditional' view, but the original draft contains a dotted line finishing at the *Victory* having headed towards the van and then turning to attack the centre – this is the track of her course as recorded by someone who actually saw it happen.

This dog-leg course also explains why it took Nelson longer to cut the line than Collingwood. As *Victory* turned to engage with her port guns whilst sailing down the line of the Combined Fleet, it provides a much more realistic opportunity for shot to cross her decks (shooting the buckle from Hardy's shoe), for the loss of her mizzen mast and for the hit to her wheel as the range closes, near to *Héros* and *Bucentaure*.

This feint also provides some justification for Dumanoir's hesitation in turning to support the centre. Even after *Victory*, *Temeraire* and *Neptune* had turned down the line, a three-decker and several 74s were still heading directly for Dumanoir's division, as well as the additional confusion caused by the *Africa* sailing down the line from the North. By the time the van did come about, it would be too late. The feint is the unique tactical feature of Trafalgar, with Nelson disguising the true point of the attack in a way never seen before in a fleet action. So why did it disappear from common understanding of the battle?

The track of the feint and the initial direction of Nelson's attack are clearly shown in Desbrière (1907), the Bridge Report (1913) and René Maine, *Trafalgar: Napoleon's Naval Waterloo* in 1955, but Rear Admiral Taylor's analysis in the

Mariner's Mirror makes no mention of it. Indeed, when this was questioned by a correspondent in 1951, Taylor responded, 'Any change of course in either direction would have delayed her [*Victory*] in getting into action. Nothing will induce me to believe that Nelson would have done this.'[21] So thorough was Admiral Taylor's analysis in most other regards that it became adopted as the de facto standard account and repeated in many later histories and biographies of Nelson. Only now is the role of the feint being recognised again.

Shortly after Collingwood broke the line in the *Royal Sovereign*, *Victory* and her consorts came into extreme gunnery range of Dumanoir's division, and all of the ships from the *Scipion* southwards record opening fire at around 12.15. At a distance of between 1,000 and 1,200 yards this had little effect on the oncoming ships. As the range closed, *Victory* turned to starboard to run down the line, opening fire with her port-side guns as she did so. The cumbersome studding sails were now cut away if they had not been shot away already – the presence of so much canvas being too much of a risk of fire in close action. *Neptune* and *Temeraire* also turned to follow *Victory*, similarly reducing sail.

12.30–13.00: Nelson's Punch through the Line

Up until this point of the battle, there was nothing to distinguish *Bucentaure*, one of several French 80s present, as the flagship of the Combined Fleet, and Nelson's attention seems to have been focused on the group surrounding the *Santísima Trinidad* as a natural point to break through.

Shortly after 12.30 Villeneuve ordered General Signal Number 5 to be flown from the *Bucentaure* – a general instruction for all ships to take station to speedily bring the enemy under fire. Still there was no specific signal for the van to come about and engage, causing the Spanish captain Churruca's famous outburst on the *San Juan Nepomuceno* that the French Admiral did not know his business: 'Perdidos! Perdidos!' – 'We are lost! We are lost!'

By 12.30 *Victory* was coming abreast of the Franco-Spanish centre, the range having reduced to a distance where the fire of this part of the Combined Fleet was taking effect (around 400–500 yards). In short order, *Victory's* mizzen mast was shot away seven feet above her deck and the wheel was destroyed, forcing her to be steered from below by chains attached directly to the tiller. This damage may have prevented Nelson's original intent of breaking the line astern of the *Santísima Trinidad*, as at no point did he single out Villeneuve's flagship as his point of attack. With steering control regained, Nelson ordered Hardy to break the line, indicating it did not matter where he did so. Hardy selected the stern of the *Bucentaure* and turned to force a way through, still under heavy fire. *Temeraire* was forced to veer to starboard to avoid colliding with *Victory* as she turned, while *Neptune* was sufficiently far behind to be able to follow in the wake of her leader. At 12.40 *Victory* broke through the line directly astern of *Bucentaure*, blasting her stern with a raking broadside before running foul of *Redoutable* to starboard.

At 11:40 Nelson had signalled, 'I intend to break through and prevent their escape to Cádiz,' but Lucas's well-drilled ship prevented *Victory* herself from doing this, both by maintaining close station in the line with *Bucentaure*, and by

Lucas's intent to fight a boarding action. *Redoutable* now grappled her much larger opponent and the two ships began to drift out of the line. Aloft, *Redoutable*'s sailors and marines set to clearing *Victory*'s top-decks with grenades and musketry, while below, *Victory*'s gunners poured round after round into their opponent.

According to James and Taylor, *Victory* was also being raked at this time from leeward by the French 80-gun *Neptune*. *Neptune*'s own log makes no mention of firing at *Victory* and it is difficult to see how she could have done so without causing significant damage to the *Redoutable*. Although her position in the line was astern of the *Bucentaure*, *Neptune*'s captain Maistral makes it clear in the log that she was not able to reach this position after the reversal of course, due to the *San Justo* blocking her progress to windward. Instead, her log mentions engaging Collingwood's flagship *Royal Sovereign* during the opening stages of the battle and it is in this position, firing with *San Justo* and *San Leandro*, that we have determined

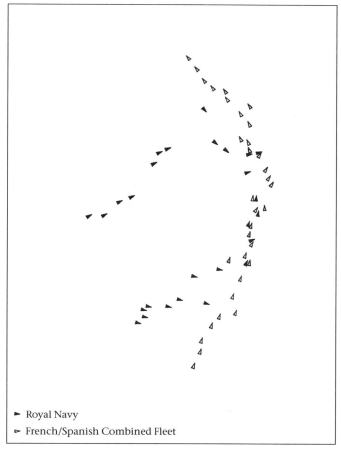

► Royal Navy
► French/Spanish Combined Fleet

Figure 2: Nelson's squadron breaks the line, 13.00

as her most likely station. Later in the battle *Neptune* would continue back down the line to engage the *Belleisle*.

Taking advantage of the gap forced by the *Victory*, the British *Neptune* was able to pass through the line at 12.50, again raking Villeneuve's flagship before turning north to engage on the leeward side as Nelson intended. *Leviathan* and *Conqueror* then also followed through, adding their weight of fire to the destruction aboard *Bucentaure*, before moving up the line on the leeward side to attack the *Santísima Trinidad*.

Temeraire had now turned back towards the line after avoiding the collision with *Victory*, but the deviation took her through the firing arcs of the group of *San Justo, Neptune* and *San Leandro*, and she began to suffer heavy rigging damage, further slowing her approach. By 13.00 Nelson's five leading ships and half of Collingwood's division had made it into action (Figure 2).

As can be seen from the diagram, Nelson's division has kept the head of the Combined Fleet's line out of the battle and has now turned to attack the centre, while Collingwood's division is fighting hard on a wide front to contain the rear. Using very different tactics and each fighting in their own way, the British Admirals are fighting a very novel battle with some real innovations. The engaged elements of the Combined Fleet are fighting fiercely and some British ships are having a very severe time of it, in particular the *Belleisle, Bellerophon* and *Colossus*.

13.00–14.00: Two Battles become One

Having sailed the length of the van of the Combined Fleet, *Africa* was now approaching the centre. *Britannia* remained standing off to windward and engaging at long range, supported by the *Ajax*. Considerable controversy remains as to the *Britannia*'s role at Trafalgar, and it is certain that Nelson did not consider Northesk as a close confidante in his plans. A family tradition within the family of Bullen, Northesk's flag captain, recalls disagreement on the quarterdeck on reducing sail too early in the action. By her own account, *Britannia* eventually passed through the line well into the battle.

In the centre, Lucas's *Redoutable* continued its efforts to board *Victory*. Ordinarily, a three-decker's additional height provided a significant advantage in any boarding contest, but in this particular instance it also reduced the distance from *Redoutable*'s fighting tops to *Victory*'s quarterdeck, and shortly after 13.15 Nelson was hit in the shoulder by a musket ball from the French ship's mizzen top, around fifty feet away.

During the Napoleonic Wars a musket ball striking the torso at such short range was almost always fatal,[22] and in Nelson's case the ball deflected downwards into his body, severed the pulmonary artery and lodged in the spine. He fell to the deck, knowing he was mortally wounded: 'They have done for me at last, Hardy – my backbone is shot through.' As casualties continued to mount on *Victory*'s upper deck, Nelson was carried below for treatment.

Returning to Collingwood's division, *Royal Sovereign* and *Santa Ana* were still battering each other into wrecks and slowly continuing to move to the north,

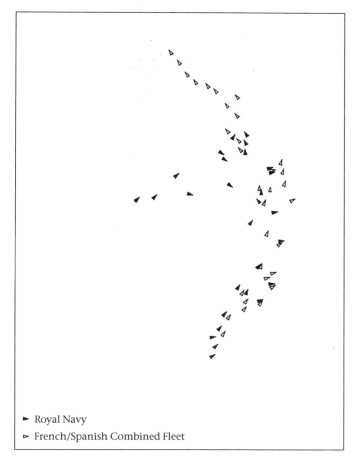

Royal Navy
French/Spanish Combined Fleet

Figure 3: The height of the action, 14.00

closing the distance to the now-drifting tangle of *Victory* and *Redoutable*. Already the two separate columns were beginning to occupy the same sea-room, with *Victory* and *Redoutable* drifting to the south-east.

Off to leeward, *Indomptable* had worn round to starboard to engage the *Belleisle* at distance, but does not appear to have taken any further significant part in the battle. As she was lost with virtually all hands in the post-Trafalgar storm, almost no account remains of her, and her role remains a blank that it may never be possible to fill. *Fougeux*, by now badly damaged by her encounters with the *Belleisle*, was moving slowly northwards toward the *Victory* and *Redoutable*.

Mars and *Pluton* had continued their running fight, and in order to avoid interfering with the duel between the *Royal Sovereign* and *Santa Ana*, found it necessary to take avoiding action. Her path to leeward blocked by the *Pluton*, *Mars* had no alternative but to turn into wind; however, this checked her progress and allowed *Pluton* to bear away and fire from astern. As Captain Duff directed the guns that could bear on her opponent from this position, he was decapitated by the *Pluton's* raking fire. *Pluton* herself then moved further ahead and engaged the *Belleisle*, now lying off to starboard.

The *Tonnant* continued locked in battle with the *Algésiras*, while the *Aigle* disengaged from the *Bellerophon* after an hour's close action, and moved up to engage on *Belleisle's* starboard side. Having skirmished with the French 74 *Achille*, *Revenge* carried on through the line and steered to the north on the leeward side. In doing so, she engaged Gravina's splendid 112-gun *Príncipe de Asturias*, emerging from the gunsmoke to starboard. Bearing away to allow her guns to bear on *Revenge*, the *Príncipe* fell away to leeward.

As we reach the height of the action at around 14.00, the rearmost ships of Collingwood's division were beginning to make their presence felt, with Durham's *Defiance* having already engaged *Príncipe de Asturias* at distance from the windward, and the *Thunderer* attacking the *Berwick*. The *Dreadnought*, *Polyphemus* and *Swiftsure* all passed astern of the *San Juan Nepomuceno*, the last ship in the line, and moved on up the line to engage from leeward. *Dreadnought* hailed *Polyphemus* to advise that she was going to engage the three-decker (ie the *Príncipe de Asturias*).

Codrington's *Orion*, in response to Nelson's instruction via frigate to engage as soon as convenient, had determined to support the part of the battle where the action was hottest by moving out of Nelson's line to cross the gap to Collingwood's division.

The 98-gun *Prince*, delayed by the need to shift a topsail, and being a slow sailor in any case, had also detached from Nelson's line and was making slow progress towards the rear of the Combined Fleet. Bringing up the rear of Nelson's division were *Spartiate* and *Minotaur*; *Spartiate* hailing the *Minotaur* to allow her to pass ahead as she was sailing faster.

14.00–15.00: The Allied Centre Falls

Shortly before 14.00 Lucas considered that *Victory's* topsides had been virtually abandoned and called for boarding parties, but just as these were assembling the *Temeraire*, most of her rigging gone and almost adrift, crashed into *Redoutable's* starboard side. With the commanding height advantage of a third deck packed with carronades, *Temeraire's* opening broadside swept *Redoutable's* decks to devastating effect, decimating the boarding parties. Caught between two three-deckers and hopelessly overmatched, Lucas had no alternative but to surrender after a truly astounding fight. Almost two-thirds of her crew were casualties, and her resistance is a matter of such national pride that a *Redoutable* has remained a named vessel in the French navy to this day.

With the true point of Nelson's attack now clear, and seeing that the van had made no move to support the centre, at 14.00 Villeneuve signalled Dumanoir to come about. There is some debate as to exactly when Dumanoir saw the signal – Villeneuve claimed to have signalled repeatedly for the van to come about in support – but whatever the truth of the matter, Dumanoir did respond to the 14.00 signal, although too late to affect the outcome of the battle.

By now the French flagship had suffered at least four point-blank stern rakes, and shortly after this signal was made, her remaining masts were shot through from below, crashing overboard. This effectively ended Villeneuve's ability to influence the battle. Robbed of central command and control, each division would now have to respond to events on its own.

With his own boats destroyed, Villeneuve hailed the *Santísima Trinidad* to send one across so he could transfer command and continue the battle, but Alava's flagship was already heavily engaged with the three-decker *Neptune*, the 74-gun *Leviathan* and the 64-gun *Africa*, which had joined the battle to take a raking position across her bows. Further to windward, *Britannia* and *Ajax* were also firing from long range.

With no prospect of response to his hails, Villeneuve ordered the colours struck to prevent further loss of life. With casualties amounting to nearly four hundred killed and wounded (according to James's *Naval History*), *Bucentaure's* resistance had been no less remarkable than that of *Redoutable*. With the colours lowered, the *Conqueror* sent a boat to take possession. Such was the pace of the battle that when the formalities of surrender were concluded, *Conqueror* had moved on northward to engage the *Santísima Trinidad* and Dumanoir's approaching van, and it was to the *Mars* that the boat carrying Villeneuve returned.

Further to the south, the stout resistance of Alava's flagship *Santa Ana* was also coming to an end. After over two hours of close action with the *Royal Sovereign*, her remaining masts finally went by the board and she surrendered with four hundred casualties. Collingwood's flagship was also virtually dismasted, requiring him to transfer his flag to the *Euryalus*.

On *Orion*, Codrington, having seen *Britannia*, *Ajax* and *Agamemnon* open fire at long range with little effect, and 'Having repeatedly pointed out the waste of shot from other ships, I now had a fine opportunity of convincing them of the benefit of cool reserve,'[23] *Orion* passed the surrendered *Santa Ana* to sweep under the stern of the French *Swiftsure* and relieve the pressure on *Colossus*, which, as we have seen, was being engaged by at least three ships.

It quickly became clear that the critical decision for the southern half of the battle during this period was to identify what happened to the *Belleisle*. The *Belleisle's* log gives a detailed account of the action around her but without ever identifying any of the other ships involved, with the exception of the British *Swiftsure*. She was in the centre of the action and engaging up to four ships at a time. Furthermore her opponents changed during the battle. For the period from 13.30, her log describes her being attacked by an enemy ship on her larboard quarter. Shortly after, a fresh ship ranged up on her starboard side. At 14.30 a third ship placed herself across *Belleisle's* starboard bow. Between 15.15 and 15.30 she was finally relieved by three British ships. We decided we had to recreate the situation around the *Belleisle* with all the evidence we could muster, because identifying the ships opposing her and the ships that relieved her was critical to fixing the position of some ships and excluding others.

Eyewitness accounts to the *Belleisle's* gallant fight are available from Lt (later Colonel) Owens[24] and Lt Nicholas Harris,[25] who served in the Marines on board. In their accounts, two of the ships attacking the *Belleisle* in this period are named as the *Achille* and the *Neptune*, and the *Polyphemus* and *Swiftsure* are the named ships providing relief. Our research, coupled with our experience of ship capabilities based on the animation up to 14.00, made us doubt some of these allocations. It should be noted that these accounts were written some considerable time after the battle and after the publication of James in the 1820s. It seemed possible that whilst the authors recalled the action, their naming of the ships could have been influenced by James's published accounts, rather than based on knowledge of the day. Had those on board *Belleisle* known their opponent's names during the action, it is likely they would have been noted in the detailed captain's log.

Our main concern was the identification of the French *Achille*. Her known original position was near the rear of the Franco-Spanish line, where she had an initial encounter with *Revenge* and *Dreadnought*. The accounts of her officers in Desbrière make it plain that she finished this encounter reduced to her two lower masts, with the rest of her rigging cut to pieces, and she was still close to the rear. She subsequently managed to turn to attack the British *Achille* and was then engaged in sequence by British ships passing up from the rear, until the *Prince* finally engaged her soon after 15.00. It is clear that she cannot have attacked *Belleisle* in the centre. In addition, the *Belleisle* mentions the later burning and explosion of the *Achille* in detached language that does not suggest that this was a ship she had encountered.

We were also not convinced about the *Polyphemus*' role, as she says nothing about the *Belleisle* in her comparatively detailed log, talking instead about supporting the British *Achille* and *Defence*. She also mentions attacking a French ship 'who took fire while we were firing on her', presumably the French *Achille*. Accepting the evidence for the *Achille*'s position therefore also placed *Polyphemus* near the rear, a position confirmed by the letter from Midshipman Reid,[26] which described her coming to the aid of the *Defence* at the rear at nearly 15.00.

This leaves us little further with identifying the ships attacking *Belleisle*. It seemed plausible that one of these was the *Neptune*; she was originally in the line near the *Bucentaure*, but in her captain's report she does not hold this station, but turns to engage the enemy's ships, which had broken the line astern of the *Santa Ana*. Plotting this course eventually brings her back to the position of the *Belleisle*. We then concluded that the French 74 fighting *Belleisle* was the *Pluton*, not the *Achille*. Accounts of both Captain Maistral on the *Neptune* and the captain of the French frigate *Hortense* place the *Neptune* and the *Pluton* together at the point where they both break off the fight. *Pluton* had earlier fought a sharp battle with the *Mars* from which she broke off on perceiving an '80-gun ship' in a threatening position astern. Her captain's account describes raking this ship several times astern and bringing down her mizzen and main topmast, both of which the *Belleisle*'s log record her losing. *Belleisle*'s topmast is recorded to fall to larboard at 14.10 – for this to have happened the wind must have been blowing from her starboard to her larboard, suggesting that by then she had drifted round to face towards the rear of the French line, away from the main direction of sail. This would leave her stern vulnerable to the *Pluton*, which we thus identified as the ship which 'laid athwart our stern', as stated in the *Belleisle*'s log, and later moved to the larboard quarter. Assuming the *Neptune* sailed past the *Belleisle* to windward, we assigned her the role of the 'Enemy ship across our starboard bow' recorded in *Belleisle*'s log at 14.30.

After some thought about times and movement, speeds and directions, working from the plots of positions we had established for 12.00, 13.00 and 14.00, we decided that the ship ranging up on the starboard side of *Belleisle* was the *Aigle*. Initially engaged with the *Bellerophon*, *Aigle* had broken off her fight by 13.30 and was regrouping, her captain and several lieutenants having been killed. The *Aigle*'s report, written by a lieutenant (Lt Classen) nearly two weeks after the battle, does not mention her engaging *Belleisle*, maintaining instead that she moved directly from engaging the *Bellerophon* to fighting the ship that was to capture her (*Defiance*, see below). However this is unlikely, given the timings of her disengagement of the *Bellerophon* (13.40) and the arrival of the *Defiance* (15.10) stated in their respective logs; it seems that there was at least forty minutes in between for a skirmish with *Belleisle*, which was perhaps forgotten after the confusion of the battle. Importantly there is a published, but apparently little-known, eyewitness account from a midshipman on the *Defiance*,[27] that after engaging the Spanish *Príncipe de Asturias* the *Defiance* was next engaged with the *Aigle*, 'one of the French ships concentrating their fire on the *Belleisle*'.

For the ships that relieved the *Belleisle*, according to her log, we have a ship taking the fire of the enemy's ship on the starboard bow (*Neptune*) at 15.15, another engaging the ship on the starboard side (*Aigle*) at 15.20, and the British *Swiftsure* (specifically named) passing the stern and taking the ship off the larboard quarter (*Pluton*) at 15.25 – although the *Swiftsure*'s log is too succinct to confirm this, essentially stating that 'there was a battle from 12.30 to 5.30 pm'. If our identification of the ship on the starboard side as the *Aigle* is correct, we know that this ship was engaged by the *Defiance* at 15.10 (according to the *Defiance*'s log) – so who drove off the *Neptune*? Here we have made an educated deduction, based on statements in the *Belleisle*'s and *Orion*'s logs, as well as the logical development of the battle animation. Nicholas Harris on the *Belleisle* describes 'a three-decker apparently steering towards us' at about 15.30. For a while there was much anxiety aboard the ship, which 'had scarce seen the British colours since one o'clock', that this 'formidable object' might be an enemy ship come to seal their fate – but to their delight she turned and they saw the British Ensign. Now, identification of ship rate in battle is often inaccurate – towards the end of the battle almost everyone in the Combined Fleet described being attacked by one or more three-deckers. However, assuming this rating is correct, there can be only one candidate, as the *Dreadnought* was the only three-decker in the rear of Collingwood's line. This ship had been fighting a running battle with the *Príncipe de Asturias* which, when plotted at 1–1.5 knots, brings her to the position of the drifting *Belleisle* at the right time.

This close association of the *Dreadnought* and *Príncipe de Asturias* and their speed of movement along the line were supported by an observation from the log of the *Orion* that at just before 14.45, shortly after aiding the *Colossus* midway along Collingwood's line, the *Orion* was unable to fire on the *Príncipe* as the *Dreadnought* was in the way. The *Príncipe de Asturias* drew level with the *Belleisle* at around

16.00, when the log of the French *Neptune* describes her and the *Pluton* steering to the assistance of Admiral Gravina. With the *Dreadnought* and *Swiftsure* coming to the *Belleisle*'s relief, *Belleisle*'s log records the *Neptune* and *Pluton* being driven off from their attack, whilst from the French point of view these two ships go to the aid of the beleaguered *Príncipe de Asturias* and enable the start of a fighting retreat. Honour is maintained all round.

Thus this reconstruction nicely ties together the positions of ships whose log and eyewitness accounts have them interacting, but which in previous reconstructions have not been placed to do so – such as the *Belleisle*, *Aigle* and *Defiance*, as well as the *Dreadnought*, *Príncipe de Asturias*, *Neptune* and *Belleisle*. The majority of the remaining battles between ships in the Franco-Spanish rear were either static or running battles taking place along the line, and thus could now be placed with reference to the position of the *Belleisle* and her opponents.

15.00–16.00: Dumanoir's Attack and the British Response

Some of Dumanoir's ships attempted to respond individually to Villeneuve's final signal for the van to engage at 14.00, before the *Formidable* finally repeated the signal at 14.30. The *Scipion* had already tried to tack on its own initiative, with the remainder of the division generally attempting to wear around, but both manoeuvres were extremely difficult due to the light winds, swell and the current. *Scipion* eventually succeeded in coming about by having her boats tow her bow through the wind, but almost another hour was lost by the time she had formed in company with *Formidable* and steered south with the *Duguay Trouin* and *Mont Blanc* (the latter two ships having collided while turning around).

Dumanoir was still intent on approaching cautiously, his course keeping his division to windward of the main battle. This was ignored by Infernet's *Intrépide*, which, in common with the *San Augustin*, headed directly for the mêlée surrounding the *Santísima Trinidad* and *Bucentaure*. This contingent of relatively fresh ships was a significant threat, but Hardy was alert to the approaching danger, as *Victory* managed to disengage from *Redoutable* and head slowly northwards. With Nelson lying mortally wounded below, Hardy was still able to exercise command and control, and signalled for a defensive line to be formed on the larboard tack to protect the heavily damaged ships in the centre.

Finding time to visit his stricken friend, Hardy reported to Nelson '. . . five of their van have tacked and show an intention of bearing down on the *Victory*. I have therefore called two or three of our fresh ships round us, and have no doubt of giving them a drubbing.'

Ajax, *Agamemnon* and *Britannia* had now finally passed through the Combined Fleet and were in position to respond to the signal, together with the *Minotaur* and *Spartiate* approaching from leeward, and those ships of the centre that were still able to manoeuvre, such as *Africa*, *Conqueror* and *Leviathan*. By 15.10 *Leviathan* lay ahead of the oncoming *San Augustin* and the two ships came together. Coming up from the south, *Orion* steered north-east in support, but after a sharp twenty-minute action *Leviathan*'s boarding party captured *San Augustin* without the need for further assistance.

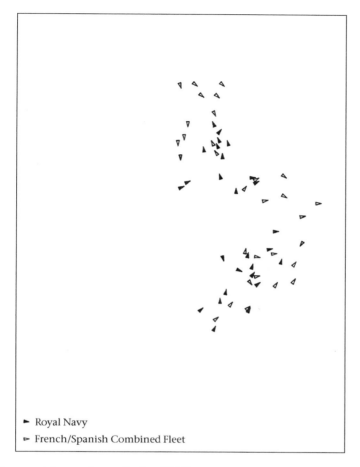

Royal Navy
French/Spanish Combined Fleet

Figure 4: Dumanoir's squadron attacks, 15.00

Intrépide's route to the centre was now blocked by the *Africa*, heading away from the dismasted *Santísima Trinidad*. As part of her role in the battle, less well known than sailing down the van, *Africa* engaged *Intrépide*, causing significant rigging damage to the larger 74. It is interesting to note that when firing to leeward against the swell British fire showed the same tendency to go high as that seen from the Combined Fleet.

Leviathan also reported engaging *Intrépide* 'warmly' with her starboard guns, supported by long-range fire from *Conqueror*. Faced with three opposing ships, *Intrépide* was forced to reduce sail at around 15.40 and defend herself. The contest between *Africa* and *Intrépide* was an unequal one – without the protection of the raking position she had enjoyed against the *Santísima Trinidad*, *Africa*'s 24-pdr main-deck guns were outmatched by *Intrépide*'s 36-pdrs, and she soon began to suffer. Fortunately *Orion* was on hand and passing to starboard of the *Leviathan*, Codrington wore his ship around the stern of the *Intrépide* at around

16.00 and moved between the French 74 and the now-silent *Africa*, shielding her from further damage. Codrington's individual conduct in seeking out the hardest-pressed British ships and coming to their aid during the battle was truly exceptional.

The farthest ship of the van, the Spanish *Neptuno*, now succeeded in wearing around and steered for the rear of Dumanoir's division to the south. As Dumanoir's division pressed on, his flagship *Formidable* came under attack from the *Minotaur* and *Spartiate* passing ahead, suffering sufficient hull damage to need to jettison several guns to survive the post-Trafalgar storm. Having crossed the head of Dumanoir's squadron, *Spartiate* and *Minotaur* now hauled round to the north to engage his succeeding ships. In this they were joined by the fire of several ships in Hardy's newly formed defensive line, with *Victory*, *Britannia* and even *Royal Sovereign* all recording firing at Dumanoir's division in their logs.

Between 15.30 and 16.00 a succession of the Franco-Spanish ships struck their colours after long struggles against their opponents. In the van, the dismasted *Santísima Trinidad* finally surrendered to the pack of surrounding ships, whilst to the rear the line completely collapsed with the badly damaged *Aigle* surrendering to *Defiance*, the *Berwick* to the *Achille* and the *San Juan Nepomuceno*, having fought several ships and suffered the death of her much-admired captain, Churruca, finally struck to the *Tonnant*.

16.00–16.30: Resolution and the Escape of Dumanoir and Gravina

By 16.00 a total of fourteen Allied ships had surrendered and Hardy was able to make his final visit to Nelson. Keenly aware of the threat to the British ships from the oncoming storm, Nelson's thoughts suddenly switched to the protection of the fleet. But Nelson's strength was soon exhausted, and at 16.30 he succumbed to the effects of his dreadful injury: *Victory*'s log recording 'a victory having been reported to the Hon. Lord Nelson, he died of his wound'.

By now Dumanoir had approached the centre of the battle, still holding his course out to windward. Confronted by a scene of shattered Allied ships and Hardy's impromptu battle line, he judged the intervention of his squadron could now achieve nothing more than the loss of further ships. Deciding to preserve his division, Dumanoir sailed on to the south.

With Villeneuve, Alava, Cisneros and now Dumanoir out of the battle, the sole remaining flag officer was Gravina in the *Príncipe de Asturias* – having duelled with the *Defiance*, *Revenge* and *Dreadnought* during the battle, he signalled a withdrawal to the north-east, in which he was supported by the efforts of the *Neptune* and *Pluton*. The remaining unengaged ships of the van, such as *Héros*, *San Francisco de Asís* and *Rayo*, had already fallen out of action to leeward and joined the overall retreat towards Cádiz. Further to the rear, ships continued to surrender. *San Ildefonso* struck to the *Defence* and the slow-sailing but powerfully armed *Prince* finally reached the line to rake the French *Achille* and set her on fire.

By 16.30 *Minotaur* and *Spartiate* had cut off *Neptuno* from reaching the rear of Dumanoir's squadron and would soon force her to surrender, and while *Intrépide* was still fighting the *Orion* at close quarters, she, too, would soon yield. *Achille*

Figure 5: The close of the action, 16.30

burned for another hour, the flames finally reaching the magazine at around 17.30 and her explosion marked the end of the Battle of Trafalgar.

A total of eighteen ships of the Combined Fleet were either destroyed or taken, with Dumanoir escaping to the south with four ships and Gravina leading eleven ships into the shelter of Cádiz harbour. As a result of the maelstrom of the post-Trafalgar storm and the astounding bravery of Cosmao-Kerjulien's sortie on 23 October to try to recover some of the prizes, very few captured ships survived to reach a British port.

Conclusions

When Nelson described his plan of attack to Captain Keats, he said 'The enemy will not know what I am about, it will bring about a pell-mell battle, and that is what I want.' While Trafalgar certainly was a pell-mell battle, Villeneuve had in fact known exactly what to expect: 'The enemy will not limit himself to forming a line of battle parallel with our own . . . he will endeavour to envelop our rear, to break through our line and to direct his ships in groups upon those of ours he has cut off, to surround them and to defeat them.' The tragedy for Villeneuve was that he was unable to conceive any effective response given the fleet he commanded.

Although accounts of Trafalgar invariably concentrate on Nelson, he was actually in command for less than ninety minutes after the start of the action. His early loss had remarkably little effect on the progress of the battle itself, as the British fleet continued to press the attack and provide mutual support for engaged ships. In contrast, the isolation of the Combined Fleet's command centre at around 13.00 caused complete tactical paralysis and disorder. By the time Dumanoir's powerful squadron had managed to engage, almost two hours later, there was nothing left of the centre to reinforce. As Nelson had predicted – 'I look with confidence to a victory before the van of the enemy could succour their friends.'

By 13.00 Nelson's job was complete. As the first flag-hoist of 'England Expects' flew during the approach, Collingwood commented testily, 'I do wish Nelson would stop signalling, we all know what it is we have to do.' There can probably be no finer unintended compliment to his friend's preparations than this remark – this clarity of communication and purpose is one of the main reasons why Nelson's methods are still studied to this day.

The 'traditional' version of Trafalgar as a heedless charge into action does not do justice to the tactical subtlety displayed by both Nelson and Collingwood. As we have seen, both commanders drew on traditions dating back over half a century to deliver the most effective coordinated attack in the history of the Age of Sail, with over half of the enemy being taken or destroyed without the loss of a single ship. The care with which Nelson ensured that his plans were communicated to his subordinates by use of personal briefings and encouragement, as well as formal orders and signals, still stands today as an example of superlative leadership. Even when Nelson himself fell, he had ensured success for the force that he commanded.

The final injustice of the 'traditional' version of Trafalgar is that is does not reflect the tremendous resistance put up by many of the ships of the Combined Fleet. With their command centre gone, individual French and Spanish ships held out against overwhelming odds, long after all reasonable hope of victory had passed.

The Battle of Trafalgar is not the story of the loss of one man. Two hundred years on, it is time for the contributions of Collingwood, Codrington, Gravina, Cosmao-Kerjulian, Churruca and, indeed, Villeneuve to take their place in the spotlight of history alongside Nelson. Above all, it is time for the bravery and sacrifice of all of those involved in the battle to be recognised. The Spanish and French crews put up fierce resistance, but their efforts were limited by isolation and a lack of cohesion, due to Nelson's plan. His was not a gung-ho charge at the enemy, but a subtle tactical manoeuvre, in which he could feel confident, as his leadership qualities had prepared the way by ensuring his intention was understood by his captains and would be willingly executed by the crews.

Post Conference Note

During the preparation of this article, a fresh contemporary account was discovered in the form of a letter written by Robert Hilton, Surgeon's Mate of HMS *Swiftsure* and published in the national press. This was of great interest as *Swiftsure*'s official log entries were sparse and the reconstruction of her course was based on deduction from other accounts rather than direct evidence. He writes:

> We were at this time nearly alongside of the enemy's lee line. The first ship that fired into us was a Spanish three-decker . . . A broadside or two from us reduced a French 80-gun ship named *L'Aigle* to the necessity of hauling down her colours. When we first fired into her, *Defiance* boarded her and were driving the Frenchmen overboard in all directions. The ship's companies crowded upon the beams, poops and quarter and every part of the ships to cheer us by giving loud 'huzzas' which we were not dilatory in returning.

The reconstruction places the Spanish three-decker *Príncipe de Asturias*, flagship of the Squadron of Observation, in position to fire on *Swiftsure* during her approach, following which *Swiftsure* doubles the rear before turning to the north.

The French *Aigle*, already 'severely handled' by her first opponent *Bellerophon*, is locked in close combat with the *Defiance* as the *Swiftsure* passes by. One can imagine that as well as cheering the *Swiftsure*, the huzzas of the *Defiance*'s company were also intended to show that *Aigle* was now under British control and that in the confusion of battle no further firing was needed.

– 2 –

'Eager and Happy to Exert Themselves in Forwarding the Public Service'

The British Fleet at Trafalgar

Colin White

O N 28 September 1805, the 100-gun British battleship HMS *Victory* arrived off Cádiz, flying the flag of Vice Admiral Horatio Lord Nelson. Inside the great bay a huge fleet of thirty-three battleships and a number of smaller craft lay at anchor. These were the ships of the combined Franco-Spanish fleet, which had taken refuge there in mid-August following the complex series of fleet manoeuvres that had finally compelled the Emperor Napoleon to call off his threatened invasion of Britain.

Although the Channel camps now lay empty and the Grande Armée was far away, deep inside Austrian territory, the Combined Fleet still posed a considerable threat and the British Government, led by Prime Minister William Pitt, was determined to deal with it. So, over the preceding month, a large British fleet had been hurriedly assembled in the waters off Cádiz, with every available battleship diverted there. On 20 August, when the Combined Fleet took refuge at Cádiz, there were just three battleships, under Vice Admiral Cuthbert Collingwood. By mid-October, no more than six weeks later, the number had swelled to thirty – an extraordinary achievement, given the communications of the time. Some had been detached from the Channel Fleet; others rushed out of the English dockyards.

It was a triumph of fleet administration – a tribute to the remarkably efficient infrastructure that Britain had created to support the Royal Navy by 1805. In the past, the credit for the excellent condition of the Trafalgar fleet has tended to be given to the First Lord, Charles Middleton, Lord Barham – certainly, the speed with which the mobilisation was carried out in those seven short weeks was due to the impetus that he gave to the whole operation. However, as Roger Knight has shown, credit must also go to Barham's predecessor, Henry Dundas, Lord Melville. It was his administration that had introduced the 'Snodgrass' system of diagonal bracing for strengthening old worn-out ships, enabling older ships to be brought back into service as harbour guard ships, and for operations in home waters – thus releasing a significant number of newer ships for foreign service.[1]

Additionally, a recently located document shows that the good condition of most of the ships that actually served at Trafalgar was also due to Melville.

Amongst his papers in the National Archive of Scotland is a list by one of his former clerks at the Admiralty, written some time after the campaign. It shows that, of the twenty-seven British battleships at Trafalgar, twenty-three of them had been docked, repaired, or brought forward during Melville's time in office. In the letter accompanying the list, the writer hoped that Melville will receive 'those congratulations to which you are so justly entitled upon the late transcendent and glorious exploit.'[2] By then, of course, Melville was facing impeachment and no such congratulations came his way.

If the British ships were in generally good condition, so too were the men. Most of the ships were sufficiently manned – although few of them had as full, or as experienced, a complement as their captains might have wished. A typical example was HMS *Tonnant*, an 80-gun former French prize commanded by Captain Charles Tyler. Thirty-five per cent of his crew were petty officers and able seamen; 25 per cent were ordinary seamen and 40 per cent landsmen and boys.[3] No doubt Tyler would have preferred a lower proportion of landsmen – but most of the French and Spanish captains could only dream of having two-thirds of their ship's company made up of experienced sailors.

The Captains

The day after the *Victory* arrived, the signal was made to the fleet 'Close around the admiral' and then, according to the ship's log, 'Vice Admiral Collingwood came on board, Sir Robert Calder and the respective captains.' About half the captains were invited on this first day – which happened to be Nelson's forty-seventh birthday – and the remainder the following day, 30 September. On each occasion there was a dinner in the splendid surroundings of the *Victory*'s Great Cabin, followed by a briefing about the admiral's plans for the battle he was certain lay ahead.

The team of commanding officers at Trafalgar was the least homogeneous that Nelson ever commanded in a major battle. Even at Copenhagen in 1801, most of the captains of the hurriedly raised fleet had served together before in the Channel or North Sea fleets. At the Nile in 1798, Nelson had not only inherited an elite team that had worked together for years, but he also had nearly two months in which to stamp his own style upon it. This time, however, he was taking command of an ad hoc fleet, hurriedly brought together from various locations.

Recently, the Trafalgar Captains have been the subject of a major research project carried out by the 1805 Club.[4] As a result, really for the first time, we have a clear idea of their background and experience. Their average age was 41. The oldest was Richard Grindall at 55; Nelson's flag captain, Thomas Hardy was 36; the youngest, at 31, was Richard King of the battleship *Achille*. They came from all over England, and from Scotland and Northern Ireland too. There were even two Americans, both of whom had been born when their states were still British colonies: Francis Laforey who hailed from Virginia and William Rutherford from Wilmington, North Carolina.

Their social background was equally diverse. At the upper end of the scale, only six were from the aristocracy. All the rest were, like Nelson, from various branches of the middle class – their fathers had been diplomats, merchants, parsons, solicitors and doctors. The father of John Cooke of HMS *Bellerophon* had been a cashier at the Admiralty. Unsurprisingly, about a third of them came from service families. Their previous experience of active service also varied considerably. A clear majority – twenty-one in all – had taken part in a fleet action before, but only six had actually commanded a battleship in a major battle.

Finally there is the question of how many had served with Nelson before. In the past, there has been a great deal of confusion about this matter; however, as a result of the new research, we can now say for certain that, of the twenty-seven commanders of battleships who eventually took their ships into action on 21 October, eleven had previously served with Nelson, either in the Mediterranean campaign of 1803–5 or in earlier campaigns.[5] In other words, more than a third, which is somewhat higher than the figures quoted in most books.

In the light of all this disparity, it is perhaps not surprising that recent research by Michael Duffy has highlighted that not all the captains performed equally well in the battle: 'Nelson had told his captains to get quickly and closely alongside an enemy, but a number who failed to do either of these obstructed the efforts of others.'[6] Moreover, now that we know exactly who had served with Nelson before, another new insight has emerged – the captains who performed best in the battle were, for the most part, men who had been with Nelson in one of his earlier campaigns. Instead of getting locked into ship-to-ship combats, like most of their colleagues, they ranged freely among the French and Spanish ships, assisting comrades who were in difficulty and, as Nelson intended, combining with other British ships to bring overwhelming force to bear on isolated ships of the enemy.

Perhaps the most striking example of this sort of fighting was the remarkable way in which the *Neptune, Leviathan* and *Conqueror* combined to knock out the key ships of the Allied centre around Villeneuve's flagship *Bucentaure*, working in concert and supporting each other.[7] The *Conqueror* was commanded by Israel Pellew and the *Leviathan* by Henry Bayntun, both of whom had served with Nelson in the Mediterranean, and HMS *Neptune* was commanded by Nelson's close friend and long-term colleague, Thomas Fremantle. Nor were they the only ones – Charles Tyler in the *Tonnant* and John Conn in the *Dreadnought* also did well, and both of them were Nelson veterans.

However, there were exceptions to the rule. On one hand, Edward Codrington of the *Orion*, who had not served with Nelson, did very well indeed. On the other, Berry of the *Agamemnon*, who had been Nelson's flag captain at the Nile, did badly – but then Berry nearly always lost his head in a crisis![8]

The Leader

So how did Nelson go about creating a team out of this disparate group? Recent analysis of his leadership methods have shown that he had a distinctive way of taking command of a new fleet;[9] he had used it in varying degrees on at least four previous occasions, so by 1805 it was well honed. His approach can be summed up in two words: entertainment and energy.

Taking entertainment first, throughout his career as an admiral, Nelson had constantly used his dining table as a means of binding his subordinates to him – but he never used it to better effect than in those busy days off Cádiz in 1805. George Duff of the *Mars* told his wife, 'I dined with His Lordship yesterday and had a very merry dinner. He certainly is the pleasantest admiral I ever served under.'[10] Codrington told his wife of 'the superiority of Lord Nelson in all these social arrangements which bind his captains to their admiral.'[11] Neither of these men had served with Nelson before and both immediately became enthusiastic supporters. Duff wrote, 'He is so good and pleasant a man that we all wish to do what he likes without any kind of orders.'

As for energy, as well as entertaining his captains, Nelson also issued them with a string of General Orders. Again, this was his customary practice whenever he took command of a new fleet – a sudden flurry of orders, each couched in his trademark urgent, emphatic language, designed to galvanise the whole fleet and get it working quickly in his way.

The recent discovery of three of Nelson's Public Order Books has enabled us to obtain fascinating glimpses of him at work in this way. These are not formal records, but workaday books designed for immediate communication and so they give us a vivid sense of how Nelson actually spoke to his subordinates.[12] For example, on 10 October alone, he issued fourteen such orders. There was his usual attention to humane detail: men sent to hospital were to have a statement of their case sent with them. His long-accumulated weatherlore was put to good use: ships were to shorten sail and get their top-gallant masts down each night, 'as gales of wind increase so suddenly in this Country'. A common identity was established by the order that, in battle, all ships were to wear the white ensign and to suspend a Union flag from the fore topgallant stay. And, as always, he demanded alertness and prompt execution of orders: 'When the Signal to Wear is made in the Night it is expected by the time the Third in Command shall have repeated the signal that the Sternmost and Leewardmost ships are before the Wind.'[13] The words 'by the time' were inserted in his own handwriting – it is clear he took a personal interest in the contents of these orders and, as was his custom, was using them as a way of continuing his dialogues with his captains. Fremantle summed up his methods neatly: 'The energy and activity on board the *Victory* will make those who are slack keep a much better look out and preserve better discipline.'[14]

However, energy and activity can be abrasive if not used carefully, so it is important also to look at Nelson's personal style – the ways in which he actually related to his captains. Once again, the newly located Order Books can help us to get closer to him than before. For example, here he is exhorting his new subordinates shortly after taking over command of the anti-invasion forces in the Channel in 1801:

As much of our success must depend on the cordial unanimity of every person I strongly recommend that no little jealousy of Seniority should be allowed to creep into our Minds but that the directions of the Senior Officer or the judicious plans of the Senior should be adopted with the greatest cheerfulness.

As it is impossible that I can be at all times in every part of my extensive Command I rely with confidence on the Judgement and Support of every Individual under my Command and I can assure them of my readiness to represent their Services in the strongest point of view to the Admiralty.[15]

It is clear that Nelson genuinely believed that cordial unanimity and cheerfulness were an essential ingredient of a successful team, and he worked hard to promote this sort of positive atmosphere in all the fleets he commanded. So, for example, he much preferred to have face-to-face meetings with his captains – dinner followed by a walk together on the quarterdeck. The two dinners on 29/30 September were not one-off events – they were followed by a series of smaller occasions when three or four captains might be invited to share a more intimate evening with their admiral. If a face-to-face meeting was not possible, a personal note – always in his own handwriting – was the next best means of communication. Many of these hasty missives have survived and they give a vivid sense of his friendly, direct and open approach.[16]

Additionally, Nelson's leadership style was essentially consultative. This was never better shown than before Trafalgar, when he consulted openly and frankly with his second-in-command, Vice Admiral Cuthbert Collingwood. Notes passed between them daily, discussing all aspects of their work, from the minute details of fleet administration to the wider strategic situation. In this case, given the shortness of the time available, Nelson was fortunate to have as his second a man with whom he had served so often before, and to whom he was so close, 'Telegraph upon all occasions without ceremony,' he told 'My dear Coll', 'We are one and I hope ever shall be.'[17]

So, the four main foundation stones of Nelson's success as a leader were:

- a strong preference for personal contact, seen in his dinners, quarterdeck walks and handwritten notes;
- an ability to galvanise and excite those who worked with him, even when dealing with the most mundane matters;
- a genuine, natural friendliness and cordiality that warmed all those who came into contact with him;
- a commitment to consultation and sharing both of his own thoughts and ideas, and the information on which those ideas were based.

One form of information in which Nelson took a keen interest, and encouraged his captains to do the same, was Intelligence. The study of Nelson's intelligence network is comparatively new – indeed, it has only really become possible with the discovery of Nelson's secret correspondence for the period 1803–5, during the course of the Nelson Letters Project.[18]

As a result, we now know that, as Nelson prepared to take on the Combined Fleets, he had some excellent intelligence material in front of him. When he arrived off Cádiz, he received a report from Henry Bayntun of the *Leviathan*, who had served with him before in the Mediterranean in 1804 and 1805, and knew well the sort of details that his chief liked. On 21 September, he had interviewed the captain of a boat that had just left Cádiz and had got some important and accurate information out of him. He told Nelson, 'There are 39 sail of the Line & frigates ready and fitting, much jealousy between the two nations – Villeneuve spoke ill of. Gravina is highly spoken of for having done his duty. The Minister Decrés[19] is expected at Cádiz to take the Chief Command.'

Bayntun had even been given some detailed reports on some of the individual ships: 'The ships in general are badly manned, the *Pluton*, *Berwick* and *Intrépide* have not more than 300 men each. He says *Aigle* is famously manned & all stout fellows.'[20] *Aigle* did indeed turn out to be 'famously manned' and her 'stout fellows' put up a splendid fight against HMS *Bellerophon*.

The Plan

By the time Nelson reached the fleet on 28 September, he already had a detailed battleplan in mind – the famous 'Nelson Touch'. Weeks earlier, he had outlined the essential points of the plan verbally to Captain Keats, while walking in the garden of the house he shared with Emma Hamilton in Merton, then a village to the south-west of London. As Keats remembered, Nelson said:

> I shall form the fleet into three Divisions in three lines. One Division shall be composed of twelve or fourteen of the fastest two-decked ships, which I shall keep always to windward or in a situation of advantage . . . I consider it will always be in my power to throw them into Battle in any part I may choose . . . With the remaining part of the Fleet formed in two Lines, I shall go at them at once . . . I think it will surprise and confound the Enemy. They won't know what I am about. It will bring forward a pell-mell battle and that is what I want.[21]

Keats's account was not written until many years afterwards, but his memory of what Nelson said has recently been confirmed by the discovery of a rough diagram scribbled on the back of some notes made by Nelson for a meeting sometime in September 1805. This shows the British attacking in three divisions with two of the divisions breaking through the enemy line while the third 'contains' them. Indeed, at one point, while demonstrating the cutting of the line, Nelson's pen has dug into the paper and made a large ink blot – a telling echo of the excitement that Keats remembered so vividly.[22]

After each of the dinners, on 29/30 September, Nelson explained this battleplan to his captains. He told Emma Hamilton that the effect was 'like an electric shock, some shed tears, all approved,'[23] but sadly, no account of what he actually said at these briefings has survived. However, on 9 October he issued a tactical memorandum outlining some of his ideas for the battle – and it seems fair to assume that it includes many of the ideas he had shared round his table ten days earlier. As it is the last plan he wrote, the temptation to see it as his final statement on the subject of tactics is very strong, and it has often been treated as such.[24] Such reverence is inappropriate. It is more helpful to see the plan as part of a continuing process – a snapshot of Nelson's thinking at the time, rather than a culmination. Recent detailed study of the six main battleplans issued by Nelson between 1798 and 1805[25] has shown that the 'Trafalgar' plan is derived from elements of its predecessors – in particular, the battleplan issued at the outset of the Nile Campaign in 1798, along with various plans issued during Nelson's period in command in the Mediterranean in 1803/4 and his subsequent chase of the French fleet to the West Indies and back in 1805.

Moreover, the plan should be seen as an essentially ephemeral document designed for a specific situation, and for specific forces. Indeed, Julian Corbett even went so far as to suggest that it was written in great hurry, at a moment when Nelson and his captains thought that the Combined Fleet was on the point of emerging.[26] There are timeless elements to it of course, but they are to be found in those parts of the plan that deal with command and communication, rather than in its tactical detail.

Let us take the tactical detail first. Like most of Nelson's earlier battleplans, this one repeatedly emphasises that his overall objective is annihilation. He wants 'to make the business decisive', and for him this means continuing the fight 'until they are captured or destroyed'. The document bristles with aggressive words: 'follow up the blow', 'over-power', 'cut through'. Indeed, reading the memorandum aloud gives a vivid sense of Nelson's speaking manner and so it probably does reflect the sort of things he said at the briefing in the *Victory*'s great cabin.[27]

To achieve this decisive result, he says he is going to divide his fleet into three divisions: two larger ones commanded by himself and Collingwood, and a smaller advanced squadron of 'the fastest sailing Two-decked ships'. His idea of separately operating divisions goes right back to the 1798 battleplan, and is a running theme through most of his subsequent plans for fleet actions. What sets the 1805 plan apart is that each division is given a distinct function. The advanced squadron has two tasks: keep the van of the enemy pinned down, so that they do not turn to help their comrades, and act as a reserve. He then says that he wants the second-in-command to 'lead through' the enemy line about the twelfth ship from their rear, while he does the same 'about their Centre'. In other words, he is planning to attack the enemy line head on – cutting through their line at right angles and breaking it into segments.

Nelson hopes that, by fragmenting the enemy line in this way, he will bring about what he had called in his conversation with Keats, 'a pell-mell battle'. By that he meant a confused maelstrom, in which the superior gunnery and seamanship of his individual ships would have the maximum advantage over their floundering, less well-trained opponents. He anticipates that by the time the van of the enemy can get round to help their comrades, the British fleet will have already won its victory, and will be in a position to fight off any counterattack.

So much for the actual fighting. Nelson is also concerned about the time that could be wasted in forming up a sailing fleet for battle. To avoid delays, he repeats a concept that he has already used in his earlier plans, 'The Order of Sailing is to be the Order of Battle.' He reinforces this by issuing an Order of Sailing and Battle with the memorandum: again, we now know that he had done this on every previous occasion.

He also insists that he wants the attack to be made as speedily as possible – ships are 'to set all their sails, even steering [studding] sails in order to get as quickly as possible to the Enemy's line'. This is contrary to usual contemporary practice in which ships tended to go into battle under reduced sail. He is doing this partly because he wants to wrong-foot his opponent – but also because a head-on attack, such as he is proposing, will expose the bows of the leading ships to the concentrated fire of the enemy. His insistence on setting all sail was designed to reduce the time his ships would take to get through the danger zone.

He also seeks to lessen the risk by introducing another new element – an idea with which he had already begun to experiment in his earlier plans, issued in the Mediterranean in 1803 and during the chase to the West Indies in 1805.[28] His Order of Battle and Sailing shows that he is planning to pack his punch, by placing some of his heaviest ships at the heads of the divisions. Not only will they be better able to stand the punishment they will receive – they will also be able to deliver a devastating first blow as they break through the line. This is exactly what happened at Trafalgar – Villeneuve remembered afterwards the 'irresistible' impression created by the sight of the three massive three-deckers at the head of Nelson's line: *Victory*, *Temeraire* and *Neptune*, bearing down on him inexorably.[29]

Nelson is therefore planning to sail into action in three divisions, each with a specific task. The divisions are each to take on part of the enemy line, breaking through at various points, creating maximum confusion and then over-powering the fragmented enemy with superior force. To minimise the risk of the head-on approach, he is going into action with all speed possible and with his biggest and most powerful units to the fore. He expects that by landing a swift and overwhelming blow like this, he will be able to defeat most of the enemy line before their excluded van can do anything to help their comrades.

Recently, it has become almost a cliché to say that the key elements of this plan were not new or revolutionary, as the old accounts of Trafalgar used to claim. Of all the various individual elements outlined above, only the massing of heavy units and the attack under full sail were genuinely new. Attack in divisions; cutting though the line; containing part of the enemy line, even the 'pell-mell' battle – all these had been tried and tested in earlier actions. However, the memorandum is also much concerned with matters of command – and it is here, above all, that its new and timeless elements are to be found.

First, Nelson devolves control of the divisions to the subordinate commanders – a concept he had introduced in his 1798 plan. Second, remarking that 'nothing is sure in a Sea Fight beyond all others', he devolves responsibility even further, passing it right down to the individual captains with the memorandum's most famous phrase: 'In case Signals can neither be seen or perfectly understood, no captain can do very wrong if he places his ship alongside that of an Enemy.' So he is prepared to trust his captains to act wisely on their own initiative – even though many of them were unknown to him.

This was a trait he showed throughout his career. Having given his subordinates a general sense of his overall aims, he was prepared to allow them freedom to carry out his orders in the way that they thought best, and he made sure that they understood this. If, as Nelson told Emma Hamilton, some of the captains really did weep with excitement when the plan was explained to them, it is more likely that it was his wonderful trust that moved them to tears, rather than the details of his tactics.

Let me nail my colours to the mast – I am convinced that if we try to reduce the 'Nelson Touch' to a precise tactical formula, we will miss its beating heart. Far better, in my opinion, to celebrate the *spirit* of the Nelson Touch – the wonderful personal leadership style that underpinned it.

The Morning of the Battle

On 2 November, Lieutenant George Hewson of HMS *Dreadnought* wrote an account of the battle for his parents. Discovered only recently, in 2004, it deserves to be better known, for it offers a vivid evocation of the scene as the great fleets sailed towards each other on the morning of 21 October:

> The human mind cannot form a grander or more noble sight. The morning was remarkably fine, the sea perfectly smooth and the lightness of the wind allowed every sail to be spread. One fleet resolutely awaited the approach, the other moved Majestically slow to the encounter . . . we went down on the enemy in line of battle ahead in two divisions by this disposition the skill of our commander was displayed, had we formed in the usual way in line of battle abreast our ships must have suffered considerably before they could have closed with the enemy, who seemed rather disconcerted at our mode of attack and not able to penetrate our designs, wore on the larboard tack to be near Cádiz in case of a defeat. Lord Nelson had so well foreseen the likely position of the enemy that he planned the manner in which every ship was to be brought into action and sent written directions to that effect to the different Captains of the fleet, so that there was no occasion for signals.'[30]

However, it would be a mistake to suppose that, once the deployment began, Nelson's task was over. As the British attack developed he was not standing back, watching as his carefully laid plans unfolded seamlessly. On the contrary, he was passionately involved and in control, right up to the moment of impact.

He maintained control in two ways. First, there were signals – both operational, such as, 'Prepare to anchor at close of day', and inspirational, as in 'England expects that every man will do his duty.' The latter is so famous that it is easy to miss just how historic a moment it was. No previous admiral had been able to 'talk' to his men in that way before – Popham's Telegraphic Code had not yet been adopted by the whole British fleet.

However, this was not the first time Nelson had used a signal to inspire his men. At the Nile, and again at Copenhagen, he had ordered Signal Number 16,

'Engage the Enemy More Closely', to be hoisted, even before the British ships were fully engaged, and then left flying throughout the battle. Clearly it was more of a battle-cry than an operational order – a reminder to his captains of what he expected of them. Now he did it again: immediately after the last flags of 'England Expects' were hauled down, they were replaced by Number 16.

Second, Nelson maintained control by sending verbal orders to individual captains – again, as he had done at the Nile and Copenhagen. Fremantle in the *Neptune* was told that Nelson intended 'to cut through the enemy's line about their 13th or 14th ship and then to make sail upon the Larboard tack for their Van'. Later, Captain Henry Blackwood of the frigate *Euryalus* was sent to the rearmost battleships in Nelson's line to repeat that they could 'adopt whatever means they thought best, provided that it led them quickly and closely alongside an enemy'.[31] So, right up to the very last moment, Nelson was still underlining his ethos, consciously echoing that key passage in the memorandum that 'no captain can do very wrong if he places his ship alongside that of an enemy.'

Most dramatic of all, Nelson was literally leading the fleet into action. The *Victory* was at the head of her line – not at all the usual position for the flagship. Nelson's officers were worried about his personal safety and made repeated attempts to persuade him to let one of the other three-deckers go ahead – attempts which he repeatedly rebuffed. Nelson's insistence on staying at the head of his line has been written off as simple recklessness by some biographers, but Nelson had an important reason for staying where he was. He did not have as many ships as he had expected and so he had not been able to create the third division to contain the enemy van and keep it pinned down and out of the action. He decided, instead, to use his own line for this purpose.

As the British attack developed, Edward Codrington in HMS *Orion* noticed that the *Victory* suddenly hauled out to port for a while, her bows pointing towards the ships in the Combined Fleet's van. Nelson had warned his captains that he might do something like this in a subsidiary memorandum to his main battleplan. This introduced a new signal ordering his ships 'to pass thro' the Enemy line as quick as possible and at the same time'. He then went on, '[t]he Admiral will probably advance his fleet to the van of theirs before he makes the Signal, in order to deceive the Enemy by inducing them to suppose it is his intention to attack their Van.' Codrington called out appreciatively to his first lieutenant, John Croft, 'How beautifully the admiral is carrying into effect his intentions!' The feint was also noticed by the French and Spanish: in a letter written shortly after the battle, Rear Admiral Dumanoir, commanding the van, said, 'The left column, having Admiral Nelson at its head, bore at first at the French vanguard.' Recently a Spanish plan of the battle was discovered in the Houghton Library at Harvard, USA, drawn by someone serving in the van, that clearly shows the *Victory* heading towards the foremost Allied ships.[32]

Having convinced the Allies that he was about to attack their van, Nelson then shifted to his real target, the centre, and thrust his way through the line astern of Villeneuve's *Bucentaure,* pouring a devastating broadside into her stern as he did so. This image of the *Victory* feinting and side-stepping like a light-footed rugby player, disguising until the last moment the place for which she was actually aiming, is most telling. It reminds us that, despite all his long-term planning, despite all the care he had taken to brief his subordinates in advance, Nelson was still able to improvise and adapt his tactics, even as the battle was unfolding.

Conclusion

As the British sailed into action on the morning of 21 October, they had well-found ships, with good-quality crews; they had a band of captains who had been inspired and knit together; and they had a concerted plan that was flexible enough to be adapted to suit the conditions they actually encountered on the day of battle. And, of course, they had a charismatic leader.

After the battle, many of those present struggled to find appropriate words to describe Nelson's leadership style. George Hewson told his parents, 'His death is greatly lamented by every person in the fleet, he had endeared himself to the seamen and officers by his humanity and conciliatory manners and in him his country has lost the greatest Adml of the age.' Collingwood told a fellow admiral, 'He possessed the zeal of an enthusiast, directed by talents which Nature had very bountifully bestowed upon him and everything seemed, as if by enchantment, to prosper under his direction. But it was the effect of system, and nice combination, not of chance.'[33]

Perhaps the best judgement came from Jane Austen's brother Francis, who had served with Nelson in the Mediterranean. Writing to his fiancée, Mary Gibson, he said:

I never heard his equal, not do I expect again to see such a man. To the soundest judgement he united prompt decision and speedy execution of plans; and he possessed in a superior degree the happy talent of making every class of persons pleased with their situation and eager and happy to exert themselves in forwarding the public service.[34]

– 3 –

Trafalgar: Myth and History

Agustín Guimera

'This battle, which has doubtless been the most tenacious and bloody ever to be witnessed by the seas . . .'

(Anonymous news, Cádiz, 1805)[1]

UNTIL RECENTLY OUR VIEW of Trafalgar had been dominated by a nineteenth-century historiography. Fortunately, in recent years, historians from Great Britain, France and Spain have been building a new approach to the three navies in conflict. In this regard, the bicentenary of Trafalgar represents a turning point in both qualitative and quantitative terms. Myths and clichés, such as the perfection and invincibility of the Royal Navy, the disunion of the leaders of the Combined Fleet and the poor Spanish–French performance during the 1805 campaign, have been called into question.

We have benefited from a more balanced study of the nature of naval warfare during the *Ancien Régime*.[2] More questions have been rasied about the strategic and tactical impact of the battle. As Nicholas Rodger has pointed out, a naval war could be won without winning battles. Any conflict in war represented a great loss for the three contenders. Despite its superiority, the Royal Navy could not guarantee everything. Great Britain had to tread a long, arduous path towards naval hegemony, which it would only attain after Waterloo. Although the British sought out decisive battle with their enemies, they always placed more value on the less obvious damage to their opponents' trade, navigation, finance, diplomacy and morale.

This chapter is divided into two parts. The first concentrates on the aspects of the 1805 campaign on which historians are in agreement. The point of departure is the idea that Trafalgar was the consequence – not the cause – of the accelerated decadence of the Spanish and French navies from 1795. The second part presents some revisionist hypotheses about Trafalgar itself, which have been put forward by various authors, and on which consensus has not yet been reached. One of these is the contention that the Combined Fleet acted in a more coordinated manner than has been claimed to date. Another hypothesis is that its performance in battle was better than had been expected by Nelson – this is linked to a series of deficiencies in various British ships, as well as to a number of errors committed by Nelson's commanders during the dramatic events of 21 October.

Concensus: The Deficiencies of the Combined Fleet

Historians are in agreement that there were major structural factors underlying the British victories between Aboukir and Trafalgar. These included the economy, finance, logistics, tactics, naval intelligence, manoeuvres and, to a certain extent, technological support. While the three nations faced identical problems in exercising naval power, by 1800 Britain had found solutions that were better suited to the naval needs of the time than its competitors. It had won the arms race and had a clear superiority; Allied shortcomings were aggravated by comparatively poor leadership. The Combined Fleet went into battle under conditions of clear inferiority, as the Spanish officers reminded Villeneuve during the famous Council of War held on 8 October in Cádiz.[3]

With its industrial revolution already underway, as well as its powerful merchant navy, the Royal Navy was numerically superior to its adversaries in 1805: more than a hundred ships of the line, compared to fifty-two in the Spanish fleet, and sixty in the French fleet. If we focus on the number of ships liable to be armed by the three maritime powers, the inequality was greater still (three to one), as Lieutenant-General José de Mazarredo, the most illustrious Spanish naval officer of the time, pointed out to Napoleon in 1800.[4] Moreover, between 1793 and 1796, Great Britain had twenty-three dry docks in its dockyards, compared to eight in France and eight in Spain. It had a higher capacity to repair and move its ships faster than its enemies.

France and Spain were maritime and land powers at the same time. Britain did not face this dilemma: the Royal Navy was seen as the protector of her insular sovereignty and the guarantor of her great international trade. The Admiralty was a powerful and effective institution supported by the nation; France and Spain did not have a centralising, operational body of this kind. This was also reflected in the naval mobilisation, although the three powers faced the same challenges when war broke out in 1803. The British were able to enlist more than 100,000 sailors, while Spain, which had a small 'Matrícula de Mar' (an official register of seamen), estimated at a maximum of 32,000 sailors in 1789, was barely able to meet the needs of almost twenty ships of the line for the 1805 campaign. The French had similar problems with their navy.

Although both sides had large contingents of soldiers at sea, Spanish and French seamen had generally been less well trained in seamanship – a structural defect related to weak trade and navigation in both nations at the time. The preventive imprisonment of French sailors by the British before the commencement of the hostilities, the blockading of their naval bases by the British as well as financial difficulties made matters worse. The French–Spanish fleets had faced several blockades over the years leading up to Trafalgar, so that even the magnificent three-deck Spanish battleship, the *Santa Ana*, which had left the Carraca dockyard in Cádiz shortly before going out to sea on 19 October 1805, sailed with its crew severely lacking physical and technical training.

Behind these shortcomings lay financial weakness. The key to a maritime power was the scope of public credit or the state's capacity to manage debt. Compared to Britain, the Spanish government at the turn of the century did not have sufficient economic resources to support the Armada. To make matters worse, greater importance was attached to the army, which was assigned the lion's share of the military budgets. The lack of financial support as well as the administrative confusion had a direct impact on the logistics that supported the navy.

However, even if more money had been available, the most important naval stores – tar, masts, ropes, etc – came from the Baltic. The northern routes were easily cut off by the Royal Navy during wartime, and local substitutes were mediocre, especially those used for rigging. The lack of good stores severely affected the Combined Fleet's capacity for manoeuvre. González-Aller Hierro and Monaque have corroborated the defects of the gunpowder that was sent with the fleet, which could not be corrected before it left Cádiz.

All this contrasted with the Royal Navy, which had built a modern logistical system during the second half of the eighteenth century. Britain was able to blockade Spain by keeping fleets at sea, supplied by a network of victualling ships that purchased fresh food and water in ports close to the Strait of Gibraltar and other posts in Portugal and Morocco. The availability of this fresh food and the generalised consumption of lemon to avoid scurvy allowed the Royal Navy to keep its fleets fitter and in better health than those of its opponents. The situation in the Combined Fleet was very different – so many men fell ill during the voyage to the Caribbean and back. Monaque cites the extreme case of the battleship *Algésiras*, which was a floating hospital by the time it reached the Galician coast in July 1805.

Technological and scientific innovation assisted the British. Nelson used the optic telegraph to communicate with his scouting frigates and battleships during the blockade of Cádiz, which provided him with up-to-date information on the movements of the Combined Fleet, right up until dawn on 21 October. The use of double-piston pumps contributed to saving the British fleet during the terrible storm that followed the battle. The Allies did not have this advantage, which contributed to the loss of various ships. Only the *Santa Ana* and *Neptuno* had this innovation. After Trafalgar, Escaño even recommended a smaller mast system so that the ships could be less exposed to breakdowns during battle and in hard weather.[5]

As regards gunnery, the large-scale use of carronades, the wider portholes and more manageable ammunition gave the British ships a major advantage in close-range fights. However, some now doubt the supposed superior rate of fire, which will be examined in the next section. Another factor for the Allies was the lack of good intelligence. Frigates were considered to be 'the eyes of the fleet' by the British. These units rendered great service to Nelson in monitoring the Allied movements. The same is not true of the Combined Fleet, which did not use enough frigates during the campaign. Frigates might have enabled Allemand's division to meet Villeneuve's fleet off Finisterre in August, which would have greatly added to the French admiral's force.

The ultimate factor in the British victory at Trafalgar was leadership. It is generally agreed that Napoleon did not understand naval warfare and bears a great deal of responsibility. The same was true of his Minister for the Navy,

Decrès, a courtier who marginalised the best naval officers. They chose Decrès's friend Villeneuve, who was an unsuitable admiral for such a complex and risky campaign.

Spanish Prime Minister Godoy was also responsible for Trafalgar. He submitted to all the Emperor's orders in order to guarantee his political survival. He subjected Gravina to constant pressure to follow Villeneuve in everything. The domineering attitude and disloyalty of France towards its ally and the weakness of Godoy prevented Gravina and his team from compensating for Villeneuve's bad tactical decisions. In contrast, the leadership displayed by the British Prime Minister, Pitt, the First Lord of the Admiralty, Lord Barham and Admiral Nelson constituted a lethal weapon against the Allies during the 1805 campaign.

At a tactical level, leadership was also crucial. It is well known that in the eighteenth century, the Royal Navy tried to overcome the tactical sclerosis of 'line-of-the-battle'. Nelson was no innovator in this regard, as these tactics had already been successfully rehearsed by Admirals Rodney, Howe and Duncan over the previous twenty years. However, Nelson is considered to be the naval leader par excellence in other ways – his focus on mutual support, flexibility and initiative among commanders was important. Nelson intended a decentralised battle by plans that had been perfectly drawn up before meeting the enemy. The Spanish and French commanders, of whom Villeneuve is the archetype, advocated more orthodox tactics: maintaining a line-of-the-battle throughout the fight; controlling the fleet's manoeuvres from the flagship and prohibiting individual initiative. However, as we shall see in part two, the Spanish had evolved towards a more flexible position after the defeat at Cape San Vincent in 1797.

Nelson's objective was to destroy the enemy. His plan at Trafalgar was to reserve his strength for short-distance fighting at pistol-shot range, overcome the enemy battleships with numerical superiority and quickly wrap up the battle without carrying out too many manoeuvres. Escaño is quite clear on this matter: 'obstinate and bloody action, which according to the instructions given in advance by the British leader to his commanders, did not commence until within shooting range and which should be decided in an hour's time at the expense of rivers of blood.'[6]

This determination contrasts with the mentality of the Allied commanders, whose sole intention was to overcome the adversary and finish the mission, without necessarily engaging in an annihilating battle. Villeneuve's tactical errors at Trafalgar are well known – his untimely departure from Cádiz, his focus on a classical line-of-the-battle, without giving Gravina's and Magon's squadrons freedom to act from a windward position to help the most needy sector of the Combined Fleet; the non-existence of a prepared and clear plan; and the order to tack towards Cádiz in front of the enemy fleet – all condemned the Combined Fleet to disaster. As for Admiral Dumanoir, the leader of the French–Spanish vanguard division, opinion remains unanimous – he took too long to decide to tack back to the battle and when he did make up his mind, he did not have the necessary wind. There are still differences of opinion regarding Gravina's conduct at the departure. This is an area to which I will refer later.

The final factor was the poor seamanship of the Combined Fleet, which resulted in the formation of an excessively long line-of-the-battle at midday of 21 October, with several battleships close together, manoeuvring in order not to collide with each other, some falling leeward. Their poor manoeuvring left spaces between several ships in an ill-formed line-of-the-battle, which could not be filled in time, with terrible consequences. From the seafaring perspective, Trafalgar was the decisive battle sought by the British, under the worst possible conditions for the Allies. Compared to the excellent performance of the Combined Fleet in Calder's action a few months previously, it may be said that the serious errors committed by Villeneuve on 21 October practically served up the victory to Nelson on a silver platter.

New Interpretations

The Napoleonic Strategy

González-Aller Hierro and various French authors claim that Napoleon's 1805 plan was practicable. The invasion of Britain could be achieved with the support of the Allied naval forces that would overcome the Royal Navy with a complex manoeuvre in the Atlantic. The plan had some advantages, such as surprise and holding the initiative, which Nelson's fruitless search for the enemy in the early months of the campaign confirms. This reflected earlier plans, such as that of Lieutenant-General Mazarredo in 1800, which demanded careful preparation and tight secrecy (in this case, the objectives were to recover Minorca and bring succour to Malta).[7]

However, I believe Admiral Monaque is right in realising that the invasion plan was unrealistic from the outset. Napoleon, with his 'land' mentality, failed to understand the winds, sea currents and weather, as well as the slow progress of a heterogeneous fleet. Uniting a fleet in the Caribbean before returning was hazardous enough, but the real Achilles' heel of the imperial plan was to ignore the British maxim of always keeping its fleet concentrated in the Western Approaches, close to the English Channel. The so-called Western Squadron had been operational since the late 1740s. If the Combined Fleet had approached the Channel it would have faced a powerful enemy. Napoleon intended to sacrifice the Combined Fleet for his military purposes.[8]

The Spanish Lieutenant-General Mazarredo, on the other hand, had constantly defended the Allied operations in the Caribbean or in the Mediterranean, far from the British bases. He opposed expeditions in the English Channel, where the enemy had logistical advantages and prevailing winds. This was made known to the French between 1799 and 1801, long before Trafalgar. I agree with González-Aller Hierro that Napoleon should have sought the destruction of British naval forces in a decisive battle, but he did not need to go into the 'lion's den' – the English Channel. The damage should have been inflicted on the Royal Navy in the distant waters of the Mediterranean, the Gulf of Cádiz or the Caribbean.

Lack of Unity in the Combined Fleet

Another myth that is now being questioned is the lack of unity among the Combined Fleet. From the outset, Decrès asked Napoleon not to use the Spanish fleet in the campaign. They both believed that one French battleship was worth two Spanish battleships. The differences in language, signals, tactics and training were compounded by the opposing ideological positions and mistrust between the officers from both nations. It has been claimed that fights were a common occurrence and that the Spanish naval officers were deemed to be cowardly and arrogant. With this biased information, it is no surprise that even today, a French author should continue to defend the same nationalistic interpretation of the events, classifying the Spanish participation as 'un cadeau empoisonné du destin'.[9]

I believe that such claims are misplaced. It was France's bad attitude to its ally since 1796 that prevented them organising successful joint campaigns – despite the great efforts made by the Spanish to honour their commitments. Excellent opportunities for mutual collaboration were lost between 1798 and 1801, such as Napoleon's expedition to Egypt or those of Bruix and Ganteume in the Mediterranean. It is true that there were ideological differences between officers, and this is a field that is worth exploring in the future. However, ideologies aside, the officer corps of both nations were formed by professionals who acted in a dignified manner, on a combined basis throughout the campaign.

In the case of the eighteen French commanders, the majority were, according to Monaque, commoners and had served in the French navy in modest posts, with limited experience in combat. Nonetheless, they acted competently in 1805 and special mention should be made of the brilliant performance of some officers, such as Lucas, Infernet and Cosmao. Among the leaders, Vice Admiral Magon contrasted with the pusillanimity of Villeneuve and the incapacity of Dumanoir. In the case of the eighteen Spanish officers that were present with Gravina at Trafalgar, many were experienced and had served well under Gravina and Mazarredo, taking part in the most important naval operations and combats of their time. Some had also taken part in the great Spanish scientific expeditions to America.

Leaders of the Spanish Fleet: Campaigns in which they participated

Algeria	1775	3
Channel	1779	4
Gibraltar*	1780	7
Pensacola	1781	2
Santa María	1782	1
Espartel*	1782	6
Algeria*	1783–4	3
Orán*	1791	3
Tolón*	1794	4
Rosas*	1794	2

Caribbean	1794	1
San Vicente	1797	3
Cádiz*	1797–9	6
Brest*	1799–1802	5
S. Domingo*	1801	2

* Participation of Gravina

Source: FP Pavía (1873), Galería biográfica de los generales de marina, jefes y personajes notables que figuraron en la misma corporación desde 1700 a 1868, Madrid, 2 vols.

The Major-General in the Spanish Fleet, Antonio de Escaño (1752–1814), was considered to be the best tactician of the eighteenth century, integrating his role in logistical and operational matters very well. His excellent organisational skills had won him the esteem and support of Mazarredo since 1779. Over the course of many campaigns, Escaño was the Second Assistant Major and then Major-General of the fleet. In the final decades of the eighteenth century, both leaders had been followed by the future heroes at Trafalgar: not only veteran leaders such as Gravina or Alava, but also officers such as Churruca, Valdés and Alcalá Galiano.

The French and Spanish leaders of the Combined Fleet had collaborated in previous campaigns, such as Bruix and Mazarredo in 1799, or Gravina and Latouche-Tréville in the blockade of Brest in the years 1799–1802, not forgetting the Santo Domingo expedition in 1801 – with the collaboration of Gravina himself – or the defence of Boulogne. The selection of Gravina as the leader of the Spanish Fleet by Napoleon and Decrès was based on his magnificent military career and his good relations with France. In short, there must have been mutual respect between the French and Spanish officers of the Combined Fleet. At the highest level, Gravina received instructions from his government to collaborate with Villeneuve at all times and that is what he did. Faced with the errors and doubts of the French Admiral, Gravina always remained loyal, even in the middle of the storm of criticism from the officers of the Combined Fleet against Villeneuve.

The defects of the Spanish battleships and particularly the training of the crews would have been mitigated to a certain extent, had the campaign started in the autumn of 1805, as Gravina wished, and not in the spring, as Napoleon rashly imposed. Tactical co-operation was ensured by signals that were agreed upon and transmitted to the fleet. However, the intercalation of French and Spanish battleships in each division of the Combined Fleet after Calder's action, at the request of Napoleon himself, encouraged closer tactical coordination at Trafalgar. As regards the morale of the Spanish Fleet, Napoleon himself acknowledged their worth after Calder's action.

The Caribbean and Calder's Action

The effective collaboration between the Allies was clear at various parts of the campaign. Spanish forces were the first to land in the seizure of the famous Diamond Rock in the Caribbean in May 1805. The decision to return to Europe, when informed of the arrival of Nelson, was a joint decision by Villeneuve and Gravina, and was a sensible one. However, the best proof of this collaboration is Calder's action – called the Battle of Finisterre in Spanish documents – which took place on 22 July.

Since the Battle of Cape St Vincent (14 February 1794), some Spanish officers had advocated tactical reform. Agustín Rodríguez has analysed the early proposals made by Mazarredo in 1776, defending the splitting of the line-of-the-battle and developing a signalling system, including those signals for a fight at pistol-shot range or night actions.[10] However, Rodríguez pays special attention to the reflections of Lieutenant-General Domingo de Grandallana between 1797 and 1804, in which he recommended following the British tactic of splitting the line to overcome the vanguard or the rearguard. This was clearly visible in the behaviour of Gravina's vanguard division during Calder's action, as a military writer from the nineteenth century described:

> On 22nd July, upon arrival at Cape Finisterre, Admiral Calder's English squadron was sighted leeward. It was heading to split the rear guard of the Combined Fleet. Gravina, who was leading the vanguard . . . tacked in the mist without being seen by the enemies; but, as they knew that if they continued their curse they would have had to fight with the entire Combined Fleet, which was higher in numbers, they also tacked when they discovered the manoeuvre. Then Gravina attacked Calder, closing him in and forcing him with the sails . . .[11]

Escaño was on board *Argonauta*, the Armada's best battleship and Gravina's flagship at head of the vanguard. Before the Combined Fleet tacked, Escaño had prepared the right signal, in case Villeneuve omitted or delayed it. The battle between half of the Combined Fleet and the whole British line took place over the course of more than four hours, surrounded by thick fog. The various manoeuvres of the *Argonauta*, the lively, accurate fire from its guns, the immediate repair of damage in the rigging and the fighting capacity of the other Spanish and French battleships involved in the battle achieved the desired result – Calder withdrew with several damaged battleships, including the three-deck battleship *Windsor Castle*.

The circumstance in which two Spanish battleships, the *Firme* and the *San Rafael*, fell into British hands was a stroke of bad luck. One of them was in poor seafaring condition, its masts and riggings useless because of damage. They fell leeward and were at risk of being captured by the enemy. The French battleship *Pluton*, under Commander Cosmao, saved another leeward Spanish battleship, the *Spain*, and tried to rescue one of them, but the lack of support from the other battleships in the rearguard meant that it had to retire. After an unequal fight, the commanders of the *Firme* and the *San Rafael* honourably surrendered.

According to Monaque, there is no evidence that Villeneuve, located in the centre of the line-of-the-battle, would have seen the difficult situation of these ships because of the thick fog. Therefore, he could not order them to be saved. However, many authors criticise his orthodox tactics and failure to allow for free initiative during the action. This prevented the rear from manoeuvring on an autonomous basis to rescue these leeward battleships. The battle could not be recommenced the following day, as Calder avoided the fight and Villeneuve lost precious time trying to organise a line-of-the-battle, instead of quickly chasing the enemy, as had been recommended by Gravina and other officers in the Combined Fleet. He also hesitated in the following days, missing a great opportunity to recover the captured battleships and inflict further damage on Calder. In spite of everything, it had been a tactical Allied victory. Escaño's role in the action was essential. It was he, according to Gravina, who had imposed order on the Spanish division and ordered the efficient tack of the entire Combined Fleet as it approached the enemy.

The Council of War (8 October) and the Departure from Cádiz

The famous Council of War in Cádiz has also attained a mythic status. The British press referred to arguments between the French and Spanish officers. Captain Churruca was said to have been present at this meeting, but in fact, the young officer was not there. The writer Quadrado y de Roo mentioned the conflict between Magon and Alcalá-Galiano, when he published a biography of Escaño in 1852, written by Vargas Ponce in 1816. However, in the latter's original manuscript this paragraph does not appear. Therefore, until new evidence comes to light, such claims should be treated with caution.[12]

At the meeting on 8 October, Escaño opposed the departure of the Combined Fleet, for reasons such as the British superiority in three-deck ships – seven compared to four, the inferiority of the Allied fleet and the greater speed of recovery of the enemy fleet from the losses in battle. He placed special emphasis on the contenders' different capacity for manoeuvre:

> He made several reflections on the difference in seafaring skills of those that were at sea with their fleets with no intermission whatsoever since the year 1793 and those that had not sailed for eight years, in particular the Spanish, who could not vouch for their seamen who were few in numbers and not very skilled.

The Combined Fleet could resist better in Cádiz by means of the famous 'subtle forces' – mostly formed by gun boats and other minor vessels that had rendered good service during the British blockades of Cádiz, Brest and Boulogne on previous occasions. Escaño also pointed out that the arrival of bad weather, which was expected, would disperse Nelson's forces. The Allies could then make the most of this to comply with Napoleon's orders and cross the Strait of Gibraltar. According to Escaño, to go to sea under the current conditions would be to head for certain disaster. The final vote favoured remaining in bay until a favourable occasion arose.[13]

Today, Cayuela and Pozuelo interpret this Council of War as a manoeuvre by Villeneuve to escape the unbearable pressure of the Emperor. With the support of his peers, the French Admiral was able to point to important reasons not to go out at that time; Escaño's intervention served his purposes.

The Departure from Cádiz

Michael Duffy argues that the departure of the Combined Fleet on 19 October was influenced by the scarcity of food in Cádiz. The fact is that the towns and villages along the bay had made a great effort to supply the Allies. I do not believe that this was the reason. The evidence points to what several French authors, such as Masson and Monaque, have called Villeneuve's 'forward flight' – a shift of mood, from doubt and pusillanimity to cold determination – which made him order the fleet to sea, contrary to what had been agreed upon on 8 October by the Council of War. Although the information received, that Nelson's forces had reduced their numbers, was influential, the truth is that Villeneuve knew that he was facing a possible unfavourable combat situation, but initiated the order to save his honour.[14]

González-Aller Hierro accuses Gravina of not having opposed Villeneuve; however, on another occasion González-Aller Hierro argues that Gravina could not act freely or suggest any tactical plan to his leader, for reasons of military subordination. He also claims that Gravina probably did not discuss the departure, thinking that the wind would not be favourable. I have argued elsewhere that Gravina was entirely restricted by his honour and his military duty to the French alliance and the Spanish government.[15]

There is another circumstance that we should explore. Sources tell us that, upon its departure from Cádiz, the Combined Fleet formed several columns and that Gravina's and Magon's observation squadron was in the most windward position. In August of that year, Gravina and Escaño had convinced Villeneuve to allow the fleet to sail in a similar formation from Ferrol to Cádiz – a battle formation in three divisions and an observation squadron in vanguard, formed by two other divisions led by Gravina. We can therefore conceive that Gravina and Escaño imagined that Villeneuve would let them operate with a certain degree of autonomy in their departure in October, as the benefits of this system had already been seen in Calder's action. However, at nightfall on 20 October, Villeneuve ordered that a single line-of-the-battle be formed. Gravina and Escaño must have been surprised by this change in attitude, but they had to accept the orders. On the morning of 21 October, Villeneuve aggravated the situation still further by ordering to tack together in front of the enemy in a short space of time. Escaño himself, the Major-General of the Combined Fleet, makes this abundantly clear in his report following the battle:

> In the end, the enemy fell onto this ill-formed line, facing to and almost entirely immobile, and attacked from very close-by, crossing through as they could, some manoeuvring to support the others as accurately and promptly as possible, manifesting their ease of manoeuvre; in which type of attack they should have had the superiority provided by their practical, well-trained fleet against ships that did not have the same training . . .[16]

In an exercise of counterfactual history, various authors have tried to evaluate the consequences of a leeward position, tacking or staying on course towards the Strait of Gibraltar. Rodríguez González claims that greater evils could have been avoided if Villeneuve had tacked leeward, keeping the order of the line-of-the-battle. Thus the Allied squadron would have moved away from the enemy, located windward, and could have reformed the line-of-the-battle. Even from this position, it would have been easier to tack towards Cádiz, as it was only a quarter-tack. He also alleges that Villeneuve could have tacked by counter march, as in Calder's action, maintaining the order of the line. This would probably have been simpler for a fleet with insufficient training and might even have frustrated any possible manoeuvre of the British.

There are also speculations that it would have been better to stay on course for the Strait of Gibraltar. In exchange for allowing the enemy to catch Dumanoir's division in the rear, Gravina's observation squadron would have been left free to manoeuvre. San Juan, on the other hand, claims that the two major errors were committed by Villeneuve – to leave Cádiz and to offer Nelson a battle with the Combined Fleet to leeward. However, it is possible that any of these evolutions would have been neutralised by Nelson's genius; he could have used one of his columns for this purpose. However, there is no doubt whatsoever that the Battle of Trafalgar would have been different, and the debate remains open.[17]

The Battle of Trafalgar

Recently, the battle has been examined anew with reference to the primary sources, such as the ships' logs, reports and correspondence of chiefs and commanders.[18] From the British perspective, Duffy has demonstrated the weaknesses in the alleged perfection of Nelson's fleet. Nelson regretted not having three months in which to transform his force into a well-oiled machine of destruction.[19] Many British commanders had not commanded a ship of the line before and only seven out of a total of twenty-seven had taken part in battle as the commanders of battleships. The fleet was well drilled in orthodox formation manoeuvres – the line-of-the-battle – but Nelson did not have enough time to instruct them regarding the new tactic of splitting the enemy line and fighting in a kind of mêlée, in which allies and enemies were mixed together.

The speed of the attack by Nelson and Collingwood, leading their columns, was not seconded by all of their commanders. The battleships that belonged to the second half of each column took a long time to join the battle – some of them with up to 170 minutes' delay – these battleships did not do their work well. Some of the British Vice Admirals also did not rise to the occasion, and failed to display sufficient initiative in such a complex, hard, tenacious fight. Duffy has also demonstrated that the gunnery training of some British battleships was not ideal; the magnificent instruction of the *Royal Sovereign*, due to Collingwood, was not the general case. To sum up, Duffy confirms that the British also made mistakes during the battle, albeit much less significant than those of their opponents.

On the other hand, the myth of universally poor Allied gunnery has been disposed of. We should not overlook the excellent gunnery performance of the Spanish vanguard at Calder's action, and there was some excellent gunnery among Allied battleships at Trafalgar, which caused major damage to the enemy.

They surrendered in the face of the enemy's superiority after several hours of fighting. Such examples can be found in the official reports of the three-deck battleships *Príncipe de Asturias, Santa Ana* and *Santísima Trinidad,* and the two-deck battleships *San Juan Nepomuceno* and the *Bahama.* Escaño is quite clear regarding Gravina's flagship:

> The officers of war, in both the Navy and the Army, the major officers, the entire infantry troop and the gunnery troop all behaved with the greatest of courage; the guns were well-served, the firing was performed on an organised basis; the cartridges were inserted with method. It is only possible to be better served by the gunnery when their assembly and tools are of the level of perfection of the enemies.[20]

Two other factors should be considered according to Agustín Rodríguez. First of all, it is known that the Spanish battleships, unlike the French, were carrying more guns than their dimensions suggested and that they were equipped with some carronades and howitzers on their decks, capable of doing great damage to the British ships. Secondly, historians have greatly exaggerated the speed of the British broadsides, because there were technical limits, such as the heating of the guns and the physical exhaustion of the crews. It is true that better gun carriages, lighter ammunition and wider portholes gave the British an advantage. The French lacked three-deck ships and carronades on deck, and, on the whole, suffered from poor gunnery training. It was for this reason that their commanders, such as Lucas, commander of the *Redoutable,* favoured the boarding technique, but the example of the manoeuvre and firing of the battleship *Pluton,* commanded by Cosmao, is a good indication that it was not so simple.

According to Agustín Rodríguez, the real difference lay in the tactical use of gunnery. The British reserved their fire until very close to the enemy battleships. They also managed to concentrate their fire by moving – three to five British battleships attacked one Allied battleship at a time. However, the decisive factor was the onslaught on the most vulnerable parts of the ship – the stern, prow and bows of the ship, especially the first one, when splitting the Allied line or rounding the enemy. Many Allied ships bore these beatings for a long time, without being able to manoeuvre to counteract them, until they surrendered.

Another aspect of the battle that has been clarified is the slight damage suffered by Nelson's fleet when approaching the Allied line. Monaque has demonstrated with calculations and diagrams that there were dead angles in the shot fired by the Combined Fleet. The time required to cross the danger zone was just ten minutes, in which time only one broadside could be made. Some ships wasted their opportunity – the ocean swell and faulty gunpowder did the rest.

The failure of the Combined Fleet to punish the approach of the British was exacerbated by the decision to tack at 08.00 on the morning of 21 October – in front of the enemy, with no time to carry it out and into the gentle wind that was blowing that day. The result was catastrophic:

The Combined Fleet should have waited for the enemy in a well-formed closed line, with a regular speed in proportion to the wind . . . a lot of time was spent putting the battleships in positions with which they weren't familiar, as after the departure from the port, the respective movement of each battleship was not noted, nor the loading and rigging changes that were necessary in order for them to move and be governed well . . . time that was needed in order to form the line well, to attain regular movement, so that, with a rotating movement, they could use their fires, *and not facing, as all the battleships were found, so that they did not form a mass, which was the reason those that the enemies attacked in order to split the line could not attack them until they were at their sides.'*[21]

The italics are mine. I think this long quotation is self-explanatory. At least seven battleships were leeward at the start of the battle or lost their position once the fight began: *Justo, Leandro, Neptune, Heros, Asis, Montañés* and *Rayo*. At 17.00, the first three battleships were to come to the rescue of the only flagship that resisted until the end, the *Príncipe de Asturias*. The remaining four joined her later on, or were able to return to Cádiz during the night.

Duffy has criticised the apparent lack of initiative of these seven battleships, but the Spanish logs and official reports confirm that they did everything they could from such a disadvantaged position. For example, the *Justo* supported the *Santa Ana* in the breaks in battle. The *Leandro* attacked the *Victory* from a distance, supporting also the *Santa Ana* from a distance. Then she luffed and drifted to avoid being attacked astern, until she could finally join Gravina. The *Montañés* attacked the *Bellephoron* astern. To quote Escaño, this vessel 'was strenuously beaten by a three-deck ship; she had to go adrift so as not to collide with two battleships and then fell leeward'. Moreover, she could not fire more effectively because two French battleships were in the way. The *Asis* could not luff or fire because two Allied ships prevented her from doing so. The other battleships, the ones that withstood the thick of the battle, played a good role, better than historians have cared to admit. They performed manoeuvres well in defence and mutual support, despite the swell, the slight wind and the poor visibility due to the smoke from the guns.

The manoeuvres of the *Príncipe* and the *Bahama* to avoid being crossed at the stern are well known. The former drifted to neutralise the enemy fire at its stern, repair damage and support the *Argonauta*. The *Trinidad* prevented the *Victory* from splitting the line at the stern of the *Bucentaure*. The *Redoutable* collided with Nelson's ship in an attempt to protect Villeneuve. The excellent seafaring conduct of the *Pluton* is another well-known fact.

There are other accounts of mutual support between the Allies, which contradict the idea of a lack of unity in the Combined Fleet. The *Príncipe*'s stern was initially defended by two battleships, one of which was the French *Berwick*. Moreover, the *Argonauta* was supported by the French *Pluton*; the *Bahama* punished the *Bellephoron*, which was engaged in battle with the *Aigle*; the *Monarca* was sustained by the *Fougueux*; and the *Leandro* and the French *Neptuno* provided one another with mutual assistance. As regards the *San Agustín,* it drifted and tacked to sustain the *Trinidad,* and its movements obliged the enemy battleships to withdraw. The most famous example is the rescue of the *Principe* at 17.00 by the battleships *Justo, Leandro* and *Neptune.* In short, the accurate manoeuvres, mutual support and tenacious gunnery defence of various Allied ships forced several British ships to withdraw, as they opted for other, easier targets. Trafalgar was won by overwhelming British superiority in the individual fights with the Allied ships that had been surrounded.[22]

Some historians have accused Gravina of not having moved his squadron from his position in the rear to assist the centre of the Combined Fleet, according to Villeneuve's demands. This is justified – there was an absence of sufficient wind, and, according to Duffy, Gravina maintained his position in order to protect the rear of Alava's division, which was suffering a severe attack from Collingwood's column at the time. Gravina's, and especially Escaño's leadership, was eventually rewarded. The *Principe* was the only flagship that had maintained this position in almost five hours of combat. However, it is true that it had lowered its flag for the fifteen minutes in which Escaño was in the infirmary. After being saved by the three aforementioned battleships, the *Principe* made the signal of union at 17.15, according to Escaño's version in the ship's log:

> At five o'clock, there was no firing to be seen on any side and the *Asís,* *Montañés* and *Rayo* were sailing to join us, when we noticed that firing had been renewed among a group of battleships on the windward side. It was ordered that all of those that were willing to engage in battle should go to sustain those that were at a disadvantage and we immediately sent out the signal to be towed to the frigate *Thémis.* The former produced no effect, because the battle ceased entirely on all sides and so the union signal was sent out at quarter past five. We continued towards Cádiz, towed by the frigate . . .

It is evident that the surviving battleships from the Combined Fleet were willing to continue the battle, but the British did not wish to fight against this group of seven Allied batteships. The Allies anchored in Cádiz that night. Of the twenty-nine Allied battleships that had entered the battle, if we subtract Dumanoir's four ships in advance, eleven had been saved, ie 37 per cent of the total. Nelson's victory may have been overwhelming, but it was not complete.

The Counterattack (23 October)

Authors acknowledge the Combined Fleet's capacity to react after the defeat at Trafalgar. Once the battle was over, the storm struck both contenders on the night of 21 October. However, the remains of the Allied fleet, anchored in the Bay of Cádiz, continued the fight two days later, in spite of the damage suffered and the bad weather. Escaño once again demonstrated his capacity for leadership. At the time, he was the most senior surviving officer in the Combined Fleet – he made the most of the first opportunity. When the storm passed on 23 October, he sent seven battleships and four frigates to rescue the ships that had been captured or that seemed to be about to sink. The log of the *Príncipe de Asturias* recounts:

[22 October] It was showery in the morning, with a gentle wind from the S. We were anchored in the port with the ships *Asís, Montañes, Rayo, San Leandro, Justo* and the French ships *Pluton, Argonaute, Neptune,* three frigates and two brigs, keeping the other two frigates sailing on the lookout. The *Héros,* which was coming towards the anchorage, was ordered to do the same. At nine o'clock, a signal was sent to call the four most senior commanders, who met on board the *Príncipe* in a meeting chaired by the Major-General, at which it was agreed that the ships that could do so should go out, in order to provide assistance and escort those that had been dismasted . . .

The departure could not be carried out that day due to the storm. The commanders themselves could not go back to their ships and were obliged to spend the night on the *Príncipe.* However, the counterattack was carried out the following day:

[23 October] It was cloudy at dawn, the horizons were stormy, the wind was NW. calm and all of the battleships were anchored. The *Algésiras* [French] was beside us, as she had watched over that night . . . At six o'clock, the commanders that had come to the meeting returned to their battleships, to gather the dismantled ships that were visible to the eye . . . At that time [ten o'clock in the morning], *Santa Ana* and *Neptuno* were already being towed by the frigates, as they had anchored at the mouth of the port, because the wind had once again shifted to the S.E., with a very poor appearance. The battleships *Rayo, Montañés, Asís, Pluton, Héros, Neptune* and *Indomptable,* with the [five] frigates continued to chase the enemies, which were escorting some of our mastless ships . . .

The British Response

At the end of the combat, the situation in the British fleet was also very difficult. The battleships suffered major damage and could not use their anchors because there were not enough cables. Collingwood wrote: 'The entire fleet was in a very critical and dangerous situation; many battleships had been left mastless and all of them had been dismantled; in thirty fathoms of water at the bottom of Cape Trafalgar . . . all of the cables had been severed cut by shots.'[23]

The statistics on the British damage, which have been published by Duffy, demonstrate that the first half of both columns had absorbed the greater share of the battle. In Nelson's column, four battleships, out of a total of twelve, had been dismantled, two of which had been left mastless and three of which needed to be towed. In Collingwood's column, which had fought with greater strength, nine battleships out of a total of fifteen had been dismantled, one of which had been left mastless and three of which needed to be towed. Both groups of battleships also suffered the majority of the fatalities and injuries in the fleet. Two commanders had died at the start of the battle and another two were seriously injured – a significant price had been paid for the victory.

In the light of the surprising departure of the Allies two days later, Collingwood ordered that a line-of-the-battle be formed between the enemy and the captured ships. The Spanish and French battleships, which had been effectively led by Cosmao, returned to port at 16.00, after rescuing two of the ships. The storm, which prevented the captured battleships from being towed, and the pressure exerted by the Allies, obliged Collingwood to take drastic measures: 'all of this delayed the towing manoeuvres and as the bad weather persisted, I determined to destroy all of them (the captured ships) that were in the most windward position . . . the probability that they might fall into the hands of the enemy . . .'[24]

Thus, at least four Allied battleships, including the *Santísima Trinidad*, which carried some seriously injured on board, were set on fire or abandoned. Of the sixteen battleships that had been captured at Trafalgar, putting aside the two battleships destroyed in the fight, only four could be towed to Gibraltar. Duffy maintains that the inadequate seamanship of the Combined Fleet caused several battleships that had survived the battle to sink in the next few days. The situation was desperate on 24 October. The strong southern winds, which had been blowing the night before, brought about a catastrophe, according to Escaño's account in the ship's log of the *Príncipe*:

The day dawned in the same way and the *Asís* and *Neptuno* were discovered stranded on the coast of Puerto de Santa María; the *San Justo* was compromised and bereft of the main and mizzen masts; the *Montañés* was in the same predicament and was missing the mizzen mast; the *Rayo* was anchored six leagues away, with an English ship at its side; and the *Indomptable* was lost in front of the *Diamante* . . . Assistance was provided to the sinking battleships and to those that were compromised and at every opportunity, the wounded were disembarked . . .

Duffy does not take into account the fact that these battleships were in a very damaged state and that, with the exception of the *Neptuno*, they did not have modern double-piston pumps. Lacking cables and having sustained substantial damage to masts and rigging, they could neither anchor nor beat out to the open sea. They were stranded close to shore and in no position to withstand the beating of the storm. Everything humanly possible had been done in an attempt to save them. While this does not entirely invalidate the claims of limited training in the Combined Fleet, it goes a long way to explain the losses. As Escaño noted on 23 October, it would have been possible to rescue more captured ships if the fleet had had greater capacity to manoeuvre.[25]

The Legacy of Trafalgar

These new interpretations of Trafalgar do not detract from the great achievements of Nelson and his commanders. On the contrary, they magnify them, as they had to face an enemy fleet that defended itself with more determination than had been expected, achieving a victory at the expense of greater efforts.

After 1805 the war continued; despite having lost many ships, officers and crews, and the major psychological impact caused by the battle, Spain still had forty-two ships of the line and excellent officers. The expenses of the campaign were absorbed by the Royal Treasury, however unwillingly. The defeat did not prevent the Spanish-American colonies from remaining loyal to the monarchy, as was demonstrated by the failed British invasions in Montevideo and Buenos Aires in 1806–7. Napoleon carried out an ambitious programme to restore his fleet and introduce other naval reforms in the following years. All was not yet lost.

The question now was whether the Armada could continue against Great Britain. In his plan to reform the Armada, drawn up in 1807, Escaño again acknowledged the great British superiority, recommending that Britain should be imitated in all aspects relating to naval affairs. He proposed radical reform at all levels.[26] However, Godoy's government did not intend to bring about the necessary reform.[27] More importantly still, time was also wanting: the Napoleonic invasion of Spain was just around the corner. After the Peninsular War, the Armada was just a shadow of its former self.

– 4 –

Trafalgar: Myth and Reality

MICHAEL DUFFY

᷉᷉᷉

THE MORE WE STUDY the Trafalgar campaign, the more it becomes clear how little we know for certain and how little we can know. The debate still continues on everything, from the extent of the original invasion threat, to what difference the battle made. As for the battle itself, much remains as hidden as it did in 1805 – by the gun smoke which shrouded the battle zone, by the deaths of so many commanders who might have explained more, and by Collingwood's determination to suppress any disputes over individual conduct.[1]

When *Royal Sovereign* and *Victory* reached the Allied line, French Lieutenant Gicquel des Touches recalled, 'The entire fleet disappeared before our eyes, enveloped by the smoke.' Lieutenant Barclay of *Britannia* recorded that, 'It became impossible to trace farther except at intervals, when the smoke cleared away *a little*.' And in the rear, the Spanish chief of staff Admiral Escaño wrote that, 'It is out of my power to furnish you with the details of these combats, it having been impossible to perceive what was going on, through the dense clouds of smoke which enveloped the Vessels, and most of those who might have made known the particulars having perished.'[2]

Casualties among senior officers were indeed among the highest since the Anglo-Dutch Wars of the seventeenth century: of thirty British admirals and battleship captains, one third were casualties, including three killed; of twenty-one French, eleven were casualties, including nine dead; and thirteen of the nineteen Spanish were casualties, of whom four died. Chief among those killed was Nelson, and the battle has become sanctified by the death of Britain's greatest admiral. But how far has this, as well as the gun smoke, obscured what actually happened and made the story of Trafalgar too Nelson-focused?

What did Nelson contribute to the battle? Firstly the immense charisma of the most victorious naval commander of his age, whose arrival gave his fleet added confidence. In the words of Henry Walker, midshipman on *Bellerophon*: '. . . though we had before that no doubt of success in the event of an action, yet the presence of such a man could not but inspire every individual of the fleet with an additional confidence. Every one felt himself more than a match for any enemy that there was any probability of being opposed to . . .'[3] The contrast between his optimism and Villeneuve's pessimism is stark.

Secondly, there was his human touch that made him adored by officers and men alike, and which was immediately put to work to raise the morale and team spirit of the fleet. And thirdly there was his aggressive tactical plan – the 'Nelson

Touch'. There is no evidence that Cornwallis, Calder or Collingwood provided any such advanced tactical guidance on their intentions to their fleets, and the Spanish complained that Villeneuve never gave any to them, but this is something that Nelson did at least three times before he did so at Trafalgar. Nelson reportedly attributed his success to always being a quarter of an hour beforehand,[4] and this is an instance of how he gained this advantage by thinking things through in advance. In comparison with Collingwood's efficient but more remote leadership, Nelson took into battle a fleet that was more confident, in better heart, and better informed than it had been before his arrival.

However, the reality was that his tactical plan did not go entirely as Nelson intended. While the numerical inferiority of the British fleet – twenty-seven of the line against thirty-three – has been used to show this as a victory against the odds, Trafalgar was a battle that everyone expected the British to win. Nine months previously, Villeneuve had told the French Minister of Marine, Decrés, that 'in reality it is utterly impossible for us to defeat the enemy when both sides are equal, indeed, they will beat us even when they are a third weaker than we are.' This may seem excessive defeatism, and there were complaints that in the cruise to the West Indies, Villeneuve had done nothing to improve his crews by training in evolutions or gunnery.

There was a general acceptance that the British were better trained, better equipped and generally better commanded than the French. Decrés frankly told Napoleon that 'our sailors, demoralised by setbacks, [are] always ready to die like heroes, but are thinking more about surrendering nobly than winning.'[5] The Spanish commanders took the same view – Admiral Alava wrote in May that their lack of sea time in the last ten years 'led to a gap between us that it would be impossible to close while we do not have the means to sail and evolve'. At the Council of War on 8 October, Escaño asserted that disaster was inevitable if they sailed.[6]

When the fleet finally left Cádiz on 20 October, the population climbed onto the rooftops and miradors to see it go, and we are told that it watched in utter silence, for fear of what might befall it if it met the British. We have to remember that Villeneuve did not sail to fight Nelson, but to get past him to Italy. He would fight if he had to force his way past, but he was hoping that detachments had reduced Nelson's fleet to only twenty-two to twenty-four ships. When on the morning of the 21st they counted twenty-seven, they were under little illusion as to what was in store.[7]

We might ask who were the braver – the British waiting to fight a larger fleet but confident of victory, or the French and Spanish coming out in the face of a fleet of superior ability, which they knew would slaughter them if it caught them. Why had they sailed at all? This was a campaign where the honour of warriors often prevailed over their reason – on both sides. Napoleon had ordered Villeneuve to sail for Italy, but then, disillusioned with his admiral's lack of vigour, sent Admiral Rosily to replace him. Hearing of this, Villeneuve decided to sail at the slightest opportunity because he could not stomach the shame of being replaced. Personal honour forced him out.

Some Spanish historians have maintained that their commander, Gravina, could have prevented the disaster by refusing to go. Again explanations have been given relating to honour – the Spanish had promised to support their hectoring ally and were honour bound to do so, and the magnificent resistance of their ships at Trafalgar has been celebrated as redeeming Spanish honour in a glorious defeat. But there were also diplomatic reasons – Spain was an empire with 'Great Power' interests, but without the force to impose on either bigger enemies or bigger friends. It had not wanted the French invasion of Britain to succeed[8] – Spain needed to keep these two larger maritime powers in balance to give it most leverage through its own navy.

In the Mediterranean, Spain did not want the French to seize control of the Kingdom of the Two Sicilies, ruled by a branch of the Spanish Bourbons. When Villeneuve was ordered to take the fleet thither, Gravina, who was Sicilian by birth, warned his Spanish masters that he would not fight against his own king, but he did not resign. Most likely he decided to accompany Villeneuve to act as a restraining force. He could have refused to sail for Italy and so stopped Villeneuve, but Villeneuve was about to be replaced by Napoleon's nominee, Rosily, who might not be so susceptible to his influence, and who had orders to sail anyway. If Spain was to protect its interests in Italy, at the very least it needed a fleet on the spot to ensure a voice at the peace table, and it was best if his colleague was still Villeneuve, with whom Gravina had established a good relationship. Gravina had a difficult role to play, and it cost him his life at Trafalgar.

In the event the Combined Fleet failed to evade Nelson and get through to Italy. However, it put up a harder fight than anyone expected, and won the respect of its opponents for doing so. As one of *Royal Sovereign*'s seamen admitted, 'they fought us pretty tightish, for French and Spanish.'[9] The British casualties at Trafalgar were far higher than in any previous battle of the Revolutionary and Napoleonic Wars, but the expected victory was also made harder for the British to win by a number of factors.

First, Nelson was seeking to raise the standard for a naval victory to new heights. In asking for more ships he wrote that 'it is . . . annihilation that the country wants, and not merely a splendid victory of twenty-three to thirty-six – honourable to the parties, but absolutely useless in the extended scale to bring Bonaparte to his marrow-bones: numbers can only annihilate.'[10] The two decisive sea battles of the Seven Years War, Lagos and Quiberon Bay in 1759, took or destroyed four ships each. In the subsequent War of American Independence, the biggest captures were in Rodney's 'Moonlight Battle' of 1780, when the Spanish lost six ships. At the Saints in 1782, the final decisive battle, four ships were captured and two more fell into British hands in the follow-up. In 1794 the Glorious First of June netted seven, in 1797 Cape St Vincent and Camperdown brought four and nine respectively, with eleven at the Nile in 1798. At Trafalgar Nelson told his officers he bargained for twenty.

Only two commanders of the age thought in terms of the annihilation of their opponent: Nelson and Napoleon. While he prayed for humanity *after* victory, Nelson was prepared to pursue victory with utter ruthlessness. Blackwood later recalled that as they sailed into action:

So much did he think of the possibility of the Enemy's escape into Cádiz, that he desired me to employ the Frigates, as much as I could, to complete the destruction of the Enemy, whether at anchor or not; and not to think of saving ships or men, for annihilation to both was his first object, and capture but a secondary one.[11]

To achieve this, Nelson was prepared to take risks that only his contempt for the Allied gunnery, and trust in his own seamen, allowed him to think of. His experience of Spanish gunnery at Cape St Vincent and French at the Nile led him to risk a head-on attack against the full broadsides of their line-of-the-battle – he needed to act fast to achieve a decisive result in the light airs and limited hours of daylight left to him on that late October afternoon. However, it meant that although he was aiming to concentrate his whole fleet against a smaller part of the Combined Fleet, to overwhelm it before the rest could intervene, in practice his own leading ships would be outnumbered as they arrived – until the rest of his fleet could arrive to support them. Everything depended on getting up quickly in close support and engaging in close action to get the results he wanted.

There was also a second obstacle to the annihilation that Nelson wanted. British historians have tended to take for granted the failings of the French or Spanish commanders and turned their own blind eye to the failings in the British performance. We need to remember that this was not Nelson's 'band of brothers', with whom he achieved his devastating victory at the Nile, hand-picked for him by St Vincent and habituated to working together by long service in the inshore squadron off Cádiz.

At Trafalgar he commanded an average British fleet of the time, hastily scratched together from various squadrons of the Channel fleet, his former Mediterranean fleet and ships newly sent out from home dockyards. They were not fully worked up either as ships or as a fleet. Five crews had been together for less than six months before Trafalgar. Nine captains had been in command of their ships for less than six months; five of these had been in command for a month or less, including two first-lieutenants made acting-captains barely a week before the battle, when their superiors went home for Calder's court-martial.

The British captains' command experience in battle was even more limited. Besides Nelson and Collingwood, only five captains had commanded a ship of the line in fleet battle before – indeed the captains of the Allied fleet were more battle-experienced, as thirteen had recently fought in Calder's action off Ferrol on 22 July, whereas only one of Nelson's captains had done so. Another two Spanish officers had commanded at St Vincent. Of the remainder of Nelson's ship-of-the-line commanders, two had commanded a ship of the line in action against a frigate, seven had commanded frigates in frigate actions, one had commanded a brig, another a bomb-ship and two a fire-ship in a battle. There is no record of six having ever been in a fleet battle. One admiral and four captains had not been in a fleet battle since the War of American Independence over twenty years before, and one (Captain Rutherford of *Swiftsure*) does not seem to have been in a battle or small ship action at all. Only eleven of the ship-of-the-line captains had served with Nelson before, and he had just over three weeks between his arrival and the battle to infuse his own tactical doctrine into them all.

Nelson employed all his communications skills to do so – over two days he had them all to dinner and explained his ideas to them. He followed this by sending them each a tactical memorandum. He provided them with a new signal with a detailed explanation of his intentions. In his memorandum he gave a fail-safe position to those who remained puzzled: 'no Captain can do very wrong if he places his Ship alongside that of an enemy.' On the day of the battle, when the desperately feeble winds made the need for haste even more apparent, he flew Signal 307, to 'make all sail possible with safety to the masts', and later number 16, to 'engage the enemy more closely'. If they were still unsure, he also sent his frigate captains to tell all the ships of the line that 'if by the mode of attack prescribed they found it impossible to get into action immediately, they might adopt whatever they thought best, *provided it led them quickly and closely alongside an enemy.*' Collingwood too was repeatedly signaling the ships of his division to make more sail.

We have tended to take it for granted that Nelson's captains did what he wanted them to do, misled by the statements of some, that they all got up as fast as they could, with all sails and studding sails set, as well as early plans of the battle which show two tight lines, all the ships correctly two cables apart. It served the interest of captured French officers who helped draw up the early plans to show they were overwhelmed by a tight mass of British warships. Historians have not changed this picture greatly since, but such tight positioning does not match the times at which the British ships actually opened fire, and there is abundant evidence to show that while the first eight of Collingwood's fifteen and the first six of Nelson's eleven got up within twenty minutes of each other, the rest came straggling into battle over the next three hours. Consequently the brunt of the battle (and most of the casualties) were borne by those first ships – which was why the battle was so prolonged and hard fought.[12]

Undoubtedly the lack of wind, and in some cases foul bottoms, played their part in the slowness of the rear ships to get up in support, but the conditions perhaps tested the seamanship of some and the initiative of others beyond their limits. Unlike in some battles of the previous war, none of the British captains did anything that might be interpreted as cowardice, nor could they be said to have been deliberately shirking. Rather they showed how widely capacities ranged to produce an average British fleet of the period. There were among them those who were excellent seamen, good fighters and ready to use their own initiative; there were those with some or one of these qualities; but there were also captains of various levels of mediocrity, and perhaps a very few who it would be flattering to describe as above bare competence. Despite all the efforts of Nelson to convey his intentions and to encourage them to act for themselves to attain them, there were those who were incapable of getting the best out of their ships and those who were reluctant to exercise their own initiative and depart from their order of sailing, in order to get up as quickly as Nelson wanted.

There were three major decisions that the British captains had to make on 21 October: (1) how to get into their correct position in the order of sailing as quickly as possible; (2) what to do in running down if held back by a slower ship in station ahead; and (3) in entering action, how to select an opponent and at what range to engage him. Each of these required seamanship skills under the prevailing wind condition, and also human decision – the use of individual initiative.

The master's logs, conveniently published together in the much-neglected 1913 Bridge Report, are illuminating on the first two of these decisions. Some were slow to get back into station early in the morning or to anticipate the signal to bear down on the enemy by having all their yards up ready to make sail. There were wide differences as to the amount of sail set and when it was set – if they had all had their sails set in the run down, there would have been no point in Nelson and Collingwood signaling to make more sail. In practice they were making as much sail as needed to keep them in station even if they could go faster than the ship ahead of them.

The two admirals tried to indicate what they needed to do by signaling *Leviathan* to overtake *Conqueror* and *Belleisle* to change places with *Tonnant*. (*Belleisle*'s log records that she did so by setting her royals and steering sails – clear evidence that faster ships were sailing with reduced canvas to keep their place in the sailing order). Some realised what was wanted and acted for themselves – Moorsom in *Revenge* pressed on ahead of those around him and was approved by signal from Collingwood for *Revenge* to make more sail. Codrington in *Orion* went off on his own, probably after receiving Nelson's message to do what he thought best to get up quickly and closely, whereas Laforey in *Spartiate*, crawling along behind the slower *Minotaur*, received Nelson's message at 13.45, but not until 15.00 did he hail *Minotaur* to pass ahead of her in order to prevent the enemy van coming to the assistance of their centre. It was not just a matter of wind conditions or foul bottoms; some captains could certainly get more speed from their ships when they wanted to, and it was a matter of judgement whether they did or not.

What then caused more problems, as Codrington found, was that in endeavouring to engage the enemy more closely, he was prevented from doing so by ships lagging in the rear, who were eager to join the fight by firing early – several times he could not get close to his intended target without being hit by the long-distance shooting of his own side. Nelson had looked for twenty captures and after the battle there were those who felt that they could have had far more if more ships had got up more quickly and engaged the enemy more closely. In the event the enemy losses in the battle totalled eighteen – three of these might have been avoided, but were the result of suicide charges by two Spanish and one French ship, plunging into the midst of the British late in the day when the battle was clearly lost, in hopeless attempts to rescue *Bucentaure* and *Santísima Trinidad*. Again considerations of honour prevailed over reason with bloody consequences.

The Allies should not take all the criticism for putting honour before reason – the parts of both Nelson and Collingwood should not go unnoticed in this respect. Each plunged into the fight at the head of their divisions. Nelson believed in leading by example, but was it honour, when he saw Collingwood surging ahead of his line, that led him to change his mind and reject the urgings of his officers to allow *Temeraire* to pass ahead of him? He put himself in the greatest danger and paid for it by losing his life and leaving his fleet without his direction for the rest of the battle.

Collingwood's concern for honour also put his division in greater difficulty. Nelson's plan had envisaged him attacking the last *twelve* enemy ships with sixteen of his own, in order to overwhelm their rear rapidly, before joining Nelson against the rest. In the event he had only fifteen with him (*Africa* had become detached overnight), and yet he attacked the *sixteenth* ship from the rear – because it was a Spanish first-rate with an admiral's flag – a foe of his own mettle. This meant that far from being a quarter superior, his division was inferior to the ships they faced, even if they all got up together, which they were far from doing – only eight got up early.

Have we therefore placed too much focus on Nelson at Trafalgar? Once Nelson and Collingwood became engaged so early and so closely, they could no longer direct their fleet. Trafalgar early on changed from being an admirals' battle to being a seamen's fight. Ultimately victory was achieved by the sheer endurance and hard fighting of the sailors and marines of the British ships earliest engaged.

The general expectations of the French and Spanish commanders as to what could be demanded from their gun crews were lower than the British, so that the British rate of fire and endurance surprised them at Trafalgar. Although the amount of gun-drill British crews received has been much exaggerated, it was still considerably better than their opponents. Spanish prisoners told the crew of the *Victory* that 'the Devil loaded the guns for it was impossible for men to load and fire as quick as we did.'[13] However, it was their endurance above all that told. Lieutenant Gicquel des Touches of *Intrèpide* wrote of broadsides which 'succeeded each other without relaxation'.[14] To quote from the log of *Revenge*, 'At 12.25, *Royal Sovereign* commenced action in the centre. At 12.35, *Revenge* commenced . . . in the rear . . . At 4.45, men firing with all expedition and spirit, having upon us four French ships and a Spanish three-decker. At 5.50 action ceased.'[15]

We tend to lose sight of this reality in the excessive focus on the death of Nelson. There is too much assumption that once *Victory* broke the line in the centre, the battle was as good as won. Moreover, the amount of column inches devoted to the engagement between *Victory*, *Redoutable* and *Temeraire* by British writers often fails to recognise the magnitude of the French *Redoutable*'s achievement. Even though his boarding tactics were a bloody failure, Captain Lucas in his 74-gun third-rate had nevertheless effectively taken a British first-rate and a second-rate out of the battle and killed the British commander-in-chief. Far less column inches are devoted to the actions of the three ships that followed through the Combined Fleet's line, *Neptune*, *Leviathan* and *Conqueror*, later helped by *Africa*, whose skilful seamanship as well as their firepower actually won the victory in the centre through their destruction of *Bucentaure* and *Santísima Trinidad*. The French general Contamine, on the receiving end in *Bucentaure*, later wrote of them:

They concentrated their fire on two or three of our ships, raking them from astern or from ahead, or firing on their quarter in such a way that our vessels, lying very nearly motionless on the water and battered moreover by far superior forces, were only able to make use of a very small proportion of their guns, and sometimes the stern-chasers alone . . . for nearly two hours they battered us, sometimes at half pistol shot.[16]

Neptune found an angle from which she could fire into the sterns both of *Bucentaure* and *Santísima Trinidad* beyond, and *Conqueror* took post close behind, her jib boom nearly touching *Neptune*'s taffrail, with the two crews cheering each other in encouragement. When *Bucentaure*'s main and mizzen masts fell, *Neptune* left *Conqueror* to finish off the now helpless French flagship and moved on to the massive *Santísima Trindidad* to repeat the process. Hercules Robinson, watching in *Euryalus*, declared 'If I were to select the most seamanlike act I witnessed I should name the *Neptune* rounding on to the quarter of the *Santísima Trinidad* and keeping the ship in command until she brought down her opponent's three masts altogether.'[17] Midshipman William Stanhope Badcock in *Neptune* told his father that 'we are not so much cut up as some of the other ships, but I believe that was owing to Captain Fremantle's good management in laying our ship alongside her opponent, and we kept up such a brisk fire that the Spanish could not keep at their guns.'[18]

Leviathan, too, 'raked and pelted [her] in a desperate manner, lying right athwart her stern' in the words of the latter's purser, and *Conqueror* also moved up in support when *Bucentaure* surrendered. When *Santísima Trinidad* surrendered, and *Conqueror* moved on to face the threatened attack from the van, one of her lieutenants, Humphrey Senhouse voiced his admiration for *Neptune*'s crew, 'who were shifting her tattered top-sails for new ones with as much coolness as if she had been in a friendly port.'[19] Here, in mutual support, skilled seamanship and sustained firepower, we have all that was best in the British performance at Trafalgar and some of the real reasons why the battle was won.

Lastly, two events heightened the impact of Trafalgar, but took place after Nelson's death and over which he had no control. One was Sir Richard Strachan's pursuit and capture of four French fugitives from Trafalgar on 4 November. This finally took the captures above the twenty wanted by Nelson and so completed the annihilation of an enemy fleet that he had sought. These four captures moreover were brought back to England long before the four saved from the post-Trafalgar storm, and this visual evidence of success made a big impact on the public mind – one of them, the *Duguay Trouin*, served the Royal Navy right up to 1949 and her stern still hangs in the National Maritime Museum. The other event was what happened in the storm that followed the battle, in which the survivors of the Combined Fleet lost more ships, while all the badly damaged British ships nevertheless survived – the impact of this was arguably as great as that of the battle itself.

In what ways was Trafalgar the 'defining moment', that became one of the bicentenary's favourite catchphrases about the battle? Nelson and his ships' companies fought for a clear purpose, which he expressed to Collingwood, 'We have only one great object in view, that of annihilating our enemies, and getting a glorious Peace for our Country.'[20] Ending the war and getting home was the dominant motivating factor for which they fought. However, Napoleon's victory over the Austrians and Russians at Austerlitz cancelled out Trafalgar, and they would have to keep fighting for another ten years. Trafalgar had no immediate impact on the war on land except to make possible the Anglo-Russian invasion of Naples – which then had to withdraw speedily after the Austrian and Russian defeat.

What difference did it make to the war at sea? If the Combined Fleet had won it would have made as little difference to the war in Europe as did British victory. It would not have renewed the immediate prospect of invasion of Britain – the Combined Fleet had been bound for Italy, not the Channel, and it would be another two years before Napoleon's army would be free to turn against Britain again. Moreover it was unlikely that the Combined Fleet would have got as far as Italy. It would have had to put back to Cádiz to repair its damages, but would have found that it had already stripped that base bare of naval stores, so that it would have been a long time before it came out again.[21] The British would have won the race to replenish first. They had six ships at Gibraltar which had not taken part in the battle and another seven shortly due from Britain, to make Nelson's fleet up to the promised forty.

What would have happened if there had been no battle? The French never sent a fleet to sea again after Trafalgar, but they were already starting to think of operating in detachments. Villeneuve had argued, and Missiessy and Allemand had demonstrated, that they operated best as small squadrons rather than as a great battlefleet. Nelson was also expecting that if they did not come out soon they would probably send out detached squadrons on raiding voyages over the winter, and that was probably accurate. Napoleon had already decided to use the Brest fleet in this way.

So what did Trafalgar achieve? It removed one source of raiding squadrons and so eased the strain on the Royal Navy's triple efforts at blockade, commerce protection and support for amphibious operations. It has been argued that the battle came just in time to save the Navy from the consequence of St Vincent's earlier ruinous conflict with the dockyards and the timber merchants, which had halted the warship-building programme and left Britain with an aging fleet. The crucial margin of superiority to fight Trafalgar had only been produced by the emergency adoption of Gabriel Snodgrass's controversial iron-bracing system, to put twenty-four otherwise unseaworthy ships to sea. There was now time to implement a proper building and repair programme, so that whereas between 1801 and 1805 the French outbuilt the British, over the next five years the British outbuilt the French. This may be so, but the Spanish had already stopped building new battleships in 1796 and however many the French built, they and the Spanish were having repair and maintenance problems of their own, particularly in the lack of naval stores. They were not really in a position to exploit St Vincent's administrative blunders.

In the end Napoleon did make up the ship losses suffered successively at Trafalgar, in Strachan's action, and at St Domingo the following February, but not only were they poorly built with inadequate materials, but the French were acutely conscious that they lacked enough experienced seamen to man them. They never again believed they could win the war at sea – they scarcely believed they could in 1805, when they were pursuing expedients to win a brief superiority in the Channel so they could launch invasion rather than seeking full fleet battle. Trafalgar and the storm that followed confirmed this view, and it forced Napoleon into seeking other ways to defeat Britain. He turned from his sailors to his army and his customs officials – to economic sanctions through his Continental System. His efforts to enforce this finally roused all Europe against him.

Amongst the first to rise against Napoleon was Spain in 1808, and its change of sides may have been facilitated more smoothly because of improved Anglo-Spanish relations in the aftermath of Trafalgar. Collingwood returned both the Spanish and French wounded directly to Cádiz and gave back all his Spanish prisoners via Gibraltar while sending the French to British prisons. In return the Spanish gave back all of the British prize crews driven ashore in the shipwrecks during the storm. These seamen all reported on how well they had been treated by the Spanish populace.

Trafalgar had long-term practical consequences; however, its most immediate and direct impact was psychological. It gave Britain the confidence and the facility to continue the war alone if necessary. However impractical were Napoleon's invasion plans, the British public had been acutely conscious that on the opposite shore of the Channel had massed the finest army in Europe. Trafalgar removed their fear that it would reach them. In the words of Prime Minister William Pitt's famous Mansion House Speech of 9 November 1805: 'England has saved herself by her exertions and will I trust, save Europe by her example.'[22]

Across the Channel the psychological impact was similar, but rested on different foundations, in which the British handling of the storm that followed the battle arguably had as great an impact as the battle itself. This was intended by Collingwood, who subsequently told the First Lord of the Admiralty, Lord Barham, that:

> I had another view in keeping the sea at that time (which had a little of pride in it), which was to show the enemy that it was not a battle, nor a storm, which was to remove a British squadron from the station they were to hold; and I have heard that keeping the sea after what had passed was a matter of the greatest astonishment to them.[23]

When Villeneuve's chief of staff, Mathieu Prigny, was later asked what act by the British Fleet had made the greatest impression on him during that battle, he replied that:

> The act that astonished me most was when the action was over. It came on to blow a gale of wind, and the English immediately set to work to shorten sail and reef the topsails, with as much regularity and order as if their ships had not been fighting a dreadful battle. We were all amazement, wondering what the English seamen could be made of. All *our* seamen were either drunk or disabled, and we, the officers, could not get any work out of them. We never witnessed any such clever manoeuvres before, and I shall never forget them.[24]

Collingwood told an old friend that:

> ... I can only say that in my life I never saw such exertions as were made to save those ships. It more astonished the Spaniards than the beating they got; and one of them said, when I assured them that none of our ships were lost 'How can we contend with such a people, on whom the utmost violence of the elements has no effect.'[25]

Two years later this was still in the mind of one of the Spanish heroes of Trafalgar, Antonio de Escaño when he asked:

> Is there any way we could compare our general way of manoeuvring with that of the English? Just take a look at some evolutions in particular and we shall be forced to admit that we have much to learn ... Do we know the secrets of dealing with storms or weighing the calms ... playing with the sea in all directions, as well as they manage it to the surprise of the world?[26]

It was not the abilities of the British commanders that continued to impress them, for Nelson was dead. Rather it was the practical lesson in the extent of British seamanship that they had just been given, and the knowledge that the numbers of trained, experienced British seamen were constantly increasing, while their own trade was at a standstill and their seamen without any but limited coastal experience, that convinced them that they could not win the naval war.

We need therefore to re-establish the British seamen alongside Nelson in perceptions of the reality of Trafalgar. Thanks to the Ayshfords' *Complete Trafalgar Roll*, we now know much more about all the seamen and marines in Nelson's fleet. There are still things we do not know – how many women were at Trafalgar and except for a very small number who have been identified, who were they? We still cannot identify how many black seamen there were at Trafalgar – how many were there in the American contingent of nearly 400 – the biggest foreign group in the fleet – or among the 164 born in the Caribbean?

However, we do have the names, ages, places of birth and other details of the vast range of seamen and marines who manned the British ships – from the solitary Chinaman, thirty-four-year-old Hampoo Hang from Canton (not the stereotypical cook or laundryman but a volunteer ordinary seaman on *Royal Sovereign*) to men such as twenty-one-year-old marine private Richard Curtis, born in Stoke Damerel, Plymouth – illiterate (he made his mark for his prize money), brown hair, fresh complexion, hazel eyes – who had enlisted in the marines when the Great War started in 1793 as a drummer (at the age of nine) and who served throughout the wars, apparently totally unscathed, until he was discharged in 1823. He was lucky – four other men at Trafalgar were born in Stoke Damerel and all four were wounded.[27]

One of these was Nelson's flag lieutenant, John Pasco. He was a man of humble origins, whose father had been a caulker in Plymouth Dockyard. He entered the navy as a captain's servant at the age of nine in 1784 and rose to master's mate in 1790 and lieutenant in 1795. He was wounded in the forearm and side by grapeshot but recovered sufficiently to take part in Nelson's magnificent state funeral. Promoted to commander for his part at Trafalgar he was eventually posted captain in 1811.

In 1846 he returned to command the *Victory* at the age of seventy-one and retired next year as a Rear Admiral. And Pasco it was, at his first Trafalgar-night dinner in *Victory*, who gave the toast to 'the immortal memory of Nelson, and those who fell with him'.[28] Over the course of time the last words of that toast were lost – the toast became exclusively to the immortal memory of Nelson. Nelson, who fought so hard after Copenhagen to get his seamen the credit they deserved, would have disapproved. It is to be hoped that in future we will commemorate the immortal memory not just of Nelson, but also of those who fell with him, and, indeed, all who served at Trafalgar.

– 5 –

Trafalgar: A French Point of View

Rémi Monaque

To French ears, the name Trafalgar always has a gloomy sound. In common language an unexpected, unjust and grievous event is still known as 'un coup de Trafalgar'. In the French navy, the battle has been, if not completely ignored, at least remembered only for the death of Nelson, who spared no love for our nation, and for the heroism of our crews, sacrificed in unequal combat. Raised in this spirit, I was somewhat hesitant to undertake the research I am about to present to you. But we should seize the occasion of the bicentenary, whilst Europe is facing difficult times, to work out together a common history, devoid of national prejudice and capable of commanding similar support in London, Paris and Madrid. I was encouraged in this endeavour by the quality of exchange I established with my British and Spanish colleagues, who have shown themselves very friendly, generous and receptive in this regard.[1]

My initial purpose was to explain the battle from the French point of view, but I do not know if such a point of view exists. I will therefore present a more modest paper – the feelings of a French naval man who has tried, sympathetically, but not complacently, to understand what his ancestors experienced.

Napoleon's Incredible Gamble

Nelson did not save England from French invasion. In fact, on 23 August, Napoleon, who the day before had still been watching out for a sight of the Combined Fleet on the cliffs of Boulogne, suddenly gave up his master plan, and decided to march the Grande Armée towards the heart of Austria. He was at this time unaware that Villeneuve had abandoned his course towards the mouth of the English Channel on 15 August, and decided to turn back to Cádiz. When Villeneuve decided to sail out of Cádiz on 18 October, he was under new orders, sending him to the Mediterranean in support of French forces engaged in the kingdom of Naples, then on to Toulon. The mission was an entirely secondary one. The tragedy of Trafalgar that evoked so much heroism and cost so many human lives was thus an unnecessary battle without any strategic stakes. How did it come to this?

Napoleon took the failure of the invasion plan he had judged unstoppable very badly. There is much to say about the weaknesses of conception and execution of this plan, but that is not the focus of this study. The Emperor was not in the habit of recognising his mistakes, and he attributed the setback he suffered to the incompetence of Villeneuve. The lengths to which he went to flay his wretched admiral were as unfair as they were outrageous: 'Villeneuve,' he wrote to Decrès, his Minister of the Navy, 'is a miserable individual, who must be shamefully thrown out. He has no strategy, no courage, no general interest, and would sacrifice everything to save his own skin.'[2]

Napoleon was determined to remove Villeneuve from his command; his way of carrying this out was astounding. The choice of a successor was not simple. The two best admirals France had when the peace of Amiens was broken in 1802, Latouche-Treville and Bruix, had been dead for a few months. Admirals with their experience and talent were not easy to find. Vice Admiral Rosily had been proposed at the time of Villeneuve's appointment, and it was to him that Napoleon turned in September 1805. This naval officer had a respectable reputation, but had never commanded even the smallest squadron, and had not been to sea since the days of the *Ancien Régime*.

On 15 September, the Emperor gave Decrès instructions for the replacement of Villeneuve. 'I believe,' he wrote, 'that two things should be done: first to send a special courier to admiral Villeneuve to order him to do this manoeuvre (to sail out of Cádiz towards the Mediterranean). Second, as his pusillanimity will prevent him from undertaking it, you will send, to replace him, admiral Rosily, who will deliver a letter ordering Villeneuve back to France to account for his conduct.'[3]

Napoleon thus made the incredible presumption that his orders would not be carried out, thus enabling him to place his new choice at the head of the Combined Fleet without alerting his disgraced predecessor. Rosily's fast arrival and discreet rallying of the fleet might have prevented the disaster. However, the admiral was held up in Madrid by some damage to his carriage and the wish of Spanish authorities to organise an escort for him on the Andalusian roads, which were infested with bandits. Villeneuve got wind of the impending arrival of his replacement. Having received no official notice of his dismissal, he deduced (quite correctly) that his friend Decrès wanted to leave him the chance to make amends. Having learned of the temporary weakening of the British blockade, he seized the first occasion that occurred to sail out. Thus, he did nothing but follow to the letter his latest instructions, which encouraged him not to remain blockaded by an inferior force, but to engage them in a 'battle of extermination'. On 8 October, a Council of War, called by Admiral Villeneuve on board the *Bucentaure*, had agreed on the impossibility of successfully fighting the British blockade, but Gravina, the commander of the Spanish squadron, did not oppose Villeneuve's plan. On 18 October, the Combined Fleet started its slow exit from the port. Two days later, after it regrouped off Cádiz, the fleet made its way towards its tragic destiny off Cape Trafalgar.

The Forces Present

In trying to understand the strengths – moral, intellectual and material – of the opposing forces at the point of confrontation, it is necessary to take a much more subtle view than many of the older histories. The balance of naval power on that day in October was far more complex than the number of vessels present, and the weight of a broadside on each side, would suggest.

The Men

It was with the cry 'Long live the Emperor!' that the crews of the French ships welcomed their admirals and captains, who shortly before the battle glumly presented them with the tricolour flag adorned with an eagle. There was enormous enthusiasm and an evident desire to fight. On Spanish vessels, similar scenes took place. It would be very unfair to explain the Combined Fleet's defeat away with a lack of patriotism and courage. It goes without saying that on the British ships, as reported by several witnesses, the desire to fight and to finish off an enemy, so long pursued, was immense. The habit of winning was even further reinforced by the calm certainty of superiority.

Amongst the more informed men, amongst all those aware of political issues, a spontaneous patriotism was enhanced by a feeling of a just cause. For the British, it was a case of protecting their country under threat, and of liberating Europe from an insatiable tyrant. The French, on the other hand, hoped to 'free the seas and the oceans of the British octopus', and spread across Europe the model for a more equal and more liberal society. Whereas the Spanish, in this adventure in spite of themselves, mused, undoubtedly without too many illusions, on the protection of their colonial empire.

So the fighters of all three nations had high morale. The best proof of this on the French side was that as soon as the sailing was announced, the sick, lying in the hospitals, rushed to the quays of Cádiz in large numbers, and managed to embark, despite doctors' orders. But beyond this communal will to fight, the professional value of the different navies was very different.

After a dozen years of almost continuous war, the composition of the British crews remained more or less satisfactory. The Admiralty still managed to furnish each ship with a hard core of real sailors – the 'top men', capable of handling the most difficult manoeuvres in any weather. The rest of the crews, though formed largely of landsmen, received valuable training during the long months at sea in the hard tasks of blockades and escorting convoys.

Having disposed of the class system, France had the advantage of a rational way of recruiting sailors without resorting to press-gangs. But her stock of mariners had run out a long time ago, and the latest call-ups had yielded ridiculously poor results. The French navy had to resort to all sorts of expedients and call on the personnel of the army. On certain ships the percentage of soldiers was close to 50 per cent. Moreover, the training these landsmen could receive was patchy. The ships that sailed from Toulon with Villeneuve had the advantage of a rather long stretch at sea, between April and August 1805, but the five vessels stationed at

Ferrol had been to sea for just the six days that took them to Cádiz. The situation was even more catastrophic for the Spanish vessels. Only one vessel, the *Argonauta*, participated in the Antilles campaign; many came from Ferrol, and the last units from Cádiz went to sea for the first time, with largely improvised crews. At the time of the Council of War held on 8 October, the Spanish admirals had declared that three of their vessels, including the powerful *Santa Ana* and *Rayo*, were only capable of sailing, not fighting.

In terms of the officer corps, France suffered from the mass emigration of the noble officers, chased away by the Revolution. However, when we specifically examine the backgrounds of the eighteen commanders at Trafalgar, compared to all the officer corps as a whole, the picture looks quite favourable. Their origins and experiences are diverse, certainly, but all had given proof of their competence, and their individual records do not give the appearance of gross deficiency.

The Tactics

Nelson's ingenious tactics undoubtedly played a large part in the extent of the British victory. However, historians have made many mistakes in their analysis of what constitutes the 'Nelson Touch'. The manoeuvre of cutting the enemy line in several parallel lines is often presented as a decisive innovation that confused the enemy. It was in fact a well-known tactic that had already been attempted by Hawke in the Battle of Cardinaux in 1759, by Rodney in 1782 at the time of the Battle of Saints, and, more recently, by Howe, in 1794 in the 'prairial' battle, which is known by the British as the 'Glorious First of June'. Besides, this manoeuvre was very dangerous when facing an enemy who could fire quickly and well. The heads of the lines present themselves perpendicular to the enemy line and are unable to fire a single shot, while remaining under heavy enemy fire for several long minutes. They risk suffering heavy losses, arriving alongside the enemy disadvantaged, and being overwhelmed by an unscathed force. However, Nelson well understood that the slowness and imprecision of the enemy's fire would leave him with the advantage. He thus took a calculated risk, adopting tactics that played on the weakness of the enemy to impose a close combat where the English carronades carried a decisive advantage.

Even more than his tactical intelligence, it was Nelson's extraordinary charisma as a leader of men that marked him out. Though most of the commanders in his fleet had never before served with him, he managed in a few days to make them understand his battleplan and communicate his enthusiasm. Thus, when the battle was at hand, the captains did not need signals to realise the admiral's plan. Admiral Collingwood, the second-in-command, led the second line into action fully understanding Nelson's intentions, using his own initiative to achieve the objectives of the day.

As for the Combined Fleet, we must recognise Villeneuve's extraordinary lucidity in describing several months beforehand how the encounter with Nelson would run. 'The enemy,' he wrote to his captains in December 1804, 'will not limit themselves in forming one line of battle parallel to bring on an artillery combat, where success often lies with the more skilled, and always with the happiest. He will seek to surround our rearguard, to pass through our line, and to close in on the isolated ships to run them down.'

Villeneuve had thus perfectly guessed the enemy's intentions. Submerged by the pessimism and paralysed by the passivity that formed the two most negative traits in his character, however, he found himself incapable of finding an original solution. He explained this very clearly in a letter to the Minister of the Navy:

> We have outmoded naval tactics, we can only get in line which is exactly what the enemy wants. I have no means, no time, and no possibility to adopt another, with the commanders to whom the vessels of the combined fleet are trusted, the majority of whom have never used their heads to reflect or have any spirit of comparison. I believe everyone will stay at their posts, but not one will be capable of taking a bold decision.

This severe assessment of his captains was not entirely justified, as could be seen from the initiative and fearlessness shown by many of them during the battle.

It was, it seems, without enthusiasm that Villeneuve decided to form a reserve or observation squadron, placed under the command of Gravina. This measure, undoubtedly suggested by the Spanish admiral and his chief of staff, Admiral Escaño, is of great interest. It divided the enormous fleet, and rendered it more manoeuvrable. The squadron, thus detached, placed windward of the main fleet, could have distracted Nelson's tactical scheme, but since the battle of 22 July, it had been decided at Napoleon's suggestion that the French and Spanish units should alternate in the formation. This was intended to reinforce the cohesion of the Combined Fleet and the solidarity between the Allies, but in practice it made any complicated manoeuvring very risky. Each ship had the added difficulty of holding her post, communicating with her neighbours and joining them in a combined effort.

The Material

If there is an area where national chauvinism has been rampant, it is naval construction. The French boast of the achievements of their great naval architect, Sané, and of having built, by the end of the eighteenth century, a very homogenous fleet of large, powerful, fast and elegant vessels. The British voice their calm assurance that they had produced vessels that were robust, well armed, capable of facing any weather and easy to maintain. The Spanish claim that they had succeeded in finding the best combination of the British and French models, making their vessels powerful, robust and fast.

An impartial observer will recognise that all three nations had reached very high standards of shipbuilding. The opponents did not hesitate to include foreign-built vessels in their fleets. Seven of Nelson's vessels in Trafalgar were of French design: three had been captured from the enemy, the *Tonnant*, the *Spartiate* and the *Belleisle*; four were directly inspired by French ship design, the *Achilles*, the *Ajax*, the *Leviathan* and the *Minotaur*. The French, for their part, sailed to the battle with two captured English vessels, the *Swiftsure* and the *Berwick*, and a Spanish one, the *Intrépide*, handed over by Madrid.

However, there was a weakness worth noticing in the Combined Fleet – their supply of wood, hemp and tar from the Baltic had long been cut off. This deficiency, notably in the solidity of masts, was particularly perceptible in the Spanish fleet where the masts were slightly oversized and insufficiently rigged. It can also be indicated that the theoretical advantage the Combined Fleet had in their greater numbers – thirty-three against twenty-seven – was compensated by the British having more large vessels. They sailed into battle with seven three-decked vessels against the four Allied, all Spanish and of varying standard.[4]

When it comes to artillery, British superiority is far more evident. British metallurgy was much more advanced than that of her rivals. At equal calibre, British canons were lighter, thus easier to manoeuvre, and put less strain on the hulls. Furthermore, the heaviest shot used by the British, the 32 (English) pounds (14.5 kg), was considerably lighter than the heaviest shot used by the Allies, weighing 36 (French) pounds (17.6 kg). The loading of the cannons was thus rendered easier and faster. Finally, the British had a decisive advantage – they had plenty of carronades at their disposal. These short, large-calibre cannons, capable of shooting out large amounts of shrapnel, proved themselves a terrible weapon in a pell-mell battle, exactly what Nelson desired. The technical advantages mentioned above were multiplied by the superior training of British gun crews. They fired more accurately, and presumably twice as quickly as their opponents.

This brief overview of the strengths and weaknesses of the participating fleets allow us to draw the following conclusions. The British fleet, though slightly smaller in numbers, was homogenous, with well-trained crews and far superior artillery, commanded by a prestigious and charismatic leader. It faced a Franco-Spanish fleet, heterogeneous by nature, with untrained and largely improvised crews, placed under the command of an admiral overwhelmed by pessimism. Under such conditions, everything pointed to a fast and easy victory for the British. However, fierce combat was needed before they could overcome their enemy.

The Encounter

At the crack of dawn on 21 October, the Combined Fleet sailed towards Gibraltar in a single, irregular line, over three and a half miles (6 km) in length. They sighted Nelson's fleet on the windward side at some ten miles' (18.5 km) distance. The British formed a disorganised mass before dividing into two lines, which, the wind behind them, steered for the centre and rearguard of the Combined Fleet's line.

At 08.00 Villeneuve ordered his fleet simultaneously to turn all vessels around. His objective, he claimed, was to protect his rearguard which was under threat. This is not a very convincing reason, as the manoeuvre only resulted in the other end of the line being menaced. It is true, in turn, that by turning towards Cádiz, the admiral approached a base where vessels in distress could find refuge. The change of tack against a strong swell and with a weak wind was a slow and difficult affair. It increased the disorder of the formation that now resembled a crescent with the hollow towards the enemy. Several vessels fell under the wind and formed into a sort of second line. Several British observers saw this configuration – which was actually the result of risky and weak manoeuvring of the Combined Fleet – as a clever defensive tactic.

Nelson, on board the *Victory*, had taken the lead in the northern line aiming towards the centre of the Allied line. On board the *Royal Sovereign*, Collingwood commanded the southern line, heading for the rearguard. With a feeble wind behind them, the two formations slowly approached the line of the Combined Fleet.

At 11.45 the *Fougueux* opened fire on the *Royal Sovereign*. The whole Allied line was soon firing, first against the southern line and, quarter of an hour later, against the northern line. The leading British vessels came under concentrated enemy fire from several vessels without being able to respond, as they only carried a few small guns in their bows. As Nelson had anticipated, the Allied artillery proved inefficient. Many shots were fired from too far and fell short; many others missed their targets. The British vessels eventually came into contact with the enemy without having suffered major damage. Passing through the line they blasted their enemies with terrible enfilades, spreading death and ravaging rigs. At short range the British carronades fired devastating loads of shrapnel. The pell-mell battle Nelson had hoped for began with incredible brutality, and fragmented into multiple individual battles.

Nelson had seemingly been menacing the Allied vanguard first, before returning towards the centre. He left it up to Hardy, his flag captain, to decide the exact point at which to break the French line. The 80-gun *Bucentaure*, Villeneuve's flagship, sailed a short distance behind the *Santísima Trinidad*, the formidable Spanish ship of 140 guns – the only one in the world to have four decks. *Bucentaure* was followed by the 74-gun *Redoutable*, which her commander, Lucas, had placed next to the admiral's vessel, having seen the space created behind her. Hardy tried to pass between these two, and then decided to engage the weaker of his two opponents. The battle that followed remains as a great achievement of the French navy.

Lucas had trained his crew magnificently for fighting. A hail of small arms fire hit the deck of the *Victory*; soon the retort of the great British vessel weakened. On his quarter deck, Nelson fell, mortally wounded by a bullet shot from the top of the mizzen mast of the *Redoutable*.[5] Lucas ordered the *Victory* to be boarded; some Frenchmen had already made their way on board. The rest of the crew prepared to leap onto the deck of the giant, but another three-decked British vessel, the *Temeraire*, appeared at the stern of the *Redoutable*, and fired a terrible enfilade on the French boarding parties. The valiant vessel continued the fight, counteracting her two powerful opponents and only lowered her flag after exhausting her last strength, surrendering to the British a ship full of dead and wounded, and in a bad condition.

The same type of scenario was repeated many times. At first encountering difficulties from the enemy's concentrated fire, the British ships were then sustained by new arrivals, and little by little they gained the upper hand. More manoeuvrable and equipped with superior artillery, the British ships succeeded in overcoming several opponents all the more easily, as certain vessels of the Combined Fleet had fallen under the wind and could only participate in the battle from afar. Several admirals' vessels, Villeneuve's *Bucentaure*, and the *Santísima Trinidad* and *Santa Ana*, fell into the hands of the enemy after fierce combat.

The salvation could have come from the ten vessels in the vanguard that had only participated in the battle from a distance. Vice Admiral Dumanoir, who commanded them, responded tardily to the order for the change of tack that Villeneuve had twice sent him. Obeyed only by four French vessels, Dumonoir wasted more time aligning the ships impeccably and ended up sailing windward of the two fleets without leading his ships to the heart of the battle. Two vessels of this formation, the *Intrépide* and the *Neptuno*, disobeyed Dumanoir's commands and made for the centre of the battle – they succumbed under the weight of enemy numbers. The others doubled back to Cádiz, joined by the survivors from the centre and rearguard, some of whom, such as the French *Pluton* and the Spanish *Príncipe de Asturias* had fought very gallantly.

The Fate of the Men

Only the British losses are known with precision. It is very difficult to find out the fate of the men in the Combined Fleet – men were killed in the battle, drowned in the shipwrecks caused by the storm that followed the battle, and died as prisoners of war. The numbers given in Table 1 are therefore estimates.

Table 1: Men Lost at the Battle of Trafalgar

	Killed	Wounded	Prisoners
French	3,499	1,138	2,200
Spanish	1,050	1,390	?
Allied Total	4,549	2,528	?
British	449	1,214	260

What is striking above all, is the small number of British casualties. The phenomenon is easy to explain. The battle, fought with unequal weapons, at times turned into massacre. What the British prize crews encountered on certain vessels was carnage. British commentators were sometimes shocked that the dead had not been thrown overboard when they arrived. They forgot that there were no longer enough men capable of disposing of the bodies. Furthermore the storm that broke out after the battle caused only a few additional losses for the British, whereas hundreds of French and Spanish were drowned.

A general account of the French men, that takes into account the battle encountered by Dumanoir's division off Cape Ortegal, is particularly tragic:

- 15,000 men, approximately, took part in the battles.
- 3,700 were killed or drowned.

- 5,300 were taken to English prisons, perhaps 3,000 returned to France with their health severely damaged.
- 2,000 were present on the vessels that were taken or sank, many of them wounded. They returned to Cádiz in different ways, many hundreds on French and British vessels from Gibraltar.
- 4,000 returned to Cádiz after the battle, aboard surviving vessels. Most of them were imprisoned by the Spanish in 1808; few survived this ordeal.

In total, barely a third of the men who fought in the battle ever saw France again. The fate of the Spanish men was less cruel, as the losses of the battle and the storm were not increased by the suffering and disappearances caused by captivity. Showing great political skill, the British immediately released all Spanish prisoners they had taken. Thus they prepared for the reforging of the alliance that three years later allowed Admiral Collingwood to present himself as a liberator in Cádiz.

Finally, there is the fate of the three commanding admirals. Their destinies are highly symbolic, as they summarise, to a certain extent, the view taken by each nation of their men who fought at Trafalgar.

For Nelson, it was a crowning moment – he was buried with great pomp in the crypt of St Paul's Cathedral. Within fifty years, his statue stood forty metres high above Trafalgar Square. He soon became the object of a near-religious cult, and the anniversary of his death is always celebrated with enthusiasm.

Gravina died of his wounds amidst his nearest friends and relatives in his hotel in Cádiz, enveloped in public admiration and even affection. His body lies in a magnificent tomb in the Pantheon of Spanish mariners of San Fernando, near Cádiz.

Villeneuve, who in vain had sought death in battle, knew captivity before perishing miserably in an inn in Rennes. He had stabbed himself in the chest six times. He was of course buried with ceremonies worthy of his position, but his grave is today unknown.

Conclusion: The Lessons of Trafalgar

Trafalgar was hardly Nelson's finest moment of glory. In this unnecessary battle, brought on by a desperate enemy's near-suicidal initiative, he benefited from a considerable margin of superiority. This does not lessen the greatness of his sacrifice or the nobility of his last moments. He will continue to be seen in international maritime history as the greatest naval personality of all times. Certain traits in his character, recently emphasised in British historiography, will, however, remain obstacles for uniform admiration among us French: his blind hatred and pronounced disrespect for our nation, his lack of cultivation and narrow-mindedness, his lasting desire to annihilate the enemy that left little place for other sentiments.

Nevertheless, the great man has left a legacy of useful lessons for all the seafarers of the world. The organisation of naval command must be simple and clear to all. In this area, British pragmatism seems to have been better suited than the complicated solutions too often adopted in France. The 'KISS' method (keep it simple, stupid), always advocated in the Royal Navy, has great virtues, especially when associated with the need to delegate to trusted subordinates. All through the Trafalgar campaign, the French admirals were given detailed and contradictory orders from the Emperor, without being sufficiently informed of Napoleon's objectives. The opposite should have applied, and Napoleon seems to have understood this, but too late.

The problem of selection, formation and the choice of leaders is essential. In these areas, the British have always given priority to practical training at sea. Their methods of selection favour, perhaps more than elsewhere, young people with naval sense and an aptitude for leadership. In this respect, Nelson is a stunning example of the detection of an outstanding precocious talent.

The subsidiary question of the relations between the leaders and their men – the team spirit – is also very important. We must not, of course, exaggerate. The French admirals and commanders were not all fierce individualists incapable of participating in a common project. Their British counterparts were not always friendly among themselves; at times they were divided by hostilities and rivalries. Nevertheless, the much boasted idea of a 'band of brothers' was more widespread in Nelson's fleet than in his opponents'. The English admiral had an aptitude for making his thoughts known and shared by his subordinates. He then trusted these men to carry out the plan without further close command.

The trust and mutual esteem that must exist between commanders of the same navy can only be acquired little by little, in the course of long periods of sailing and training. In this respect, the British superiority was very clear. So many of the French and Spanish officer corps and seamen lacked sea time. It must be noted that in the Combined Fleet many of the outstanding feats were individual actions. Certain commanders had, despite the circumstances, succeeded in giving their crews remarkable training and morale. Their exploits remind us that even in the worst conditions, enthusiasm, optimism and obstinacy can work miracles. Courage, a sense of honour and love of one's country were also powerful motives that invigorated the fighters of all three nations.

However, we cannot count on surges of heroism to win a battle. Progressive, rational and realistic preparation is indispensable. This is perhaps what the British understood before the others. Their training centres are often models for realism and harshness of methods. These days, in all developed countries, strict procedures are employed to ensure the operational capability of vessels before sending them on a mission. We are a long way from the tragic lack of preparation for certain crews that were thrown into the furnace of Trafalgar.

Behind the Wooden Walls

The British Defences Against Invasion, 1803–1805

Clive Emsley

I N NINETEENTH-CENTURY BRITAIN, AND up until 1914, the conflict against the French Revolution and Napoleonic France was commonly described as 'the Great War'. Although a latecomer into the war against Revolutionary France, Britain became France's most persistent enemy for almost a quarter of a century of fighting (1793–1815). Britain's effort in the wars was colossal. While her population was much smaller than that of France – especially a France swollen by imperial conquest – her economy was pulling ahead and her fiscal system was considerably superior. These economic advantages enabled Britain to play a role similar to that of the United States in the Second World War, that is as both key combatant and also the arsenal, lynchpin and, in particular, financier of a succession of continental coalitions.

During the first stage of the conflict, from 1793 to the turn of the century, the British government's war aims were confused. Ministers argued and took up different positions. Should they continue the eighteenth-century policy of focussing their main efforts against French colonies? Should they seek to restore the French monarchy and focus their attention on Europe? Should they be prepared to make peace with the republican government? And throughout the arguments over war aims, there remained a constant, nagging anxiety about a French invasion attempt possibly linking up with revolutionary radicals in Britain. Some French invasion attempts were aborted, most notably Lazare Hoche's expedition to Bantry Bay in December 1796. In February 1797, however, a small body of poorly trained troops successfully landed in Wales and, while it surrendered almost immediately, it still caused panic and a run on the banks. In the following year a thousand veterans of Citizen General Bonaparte's Army of Italy landed to support the Irish rebellion. General Humbert's men acquitted themselves well until, heavily outnumbered and running low on supplies, they surrendered to General Lake at Ballinamuck and left their Irish peasant allies to the destructive power of British artillery and volley fire.[1]

A brief period of peace followed the signing of the preliminary treaty of London in October 1801 initially, and then the Peace of Amiens in May 1802. Dislike, distrust and the laggard implementation of requirements of the peace by both sides soon brought about its rupture. War resumed in May 1803, and over the following two years British anxiety about invasion reached a peak. From the early summer of 1803 Boulogne, chosen as the launch point for Napoleon's intended invasion, became a hive of activity. New quays were built; ships were collected; eventually, some 190,000 men were quartered in and around the town, all in preparation for the great enterprise. Then, at the end of August 1805, with a threat brewing in central Europe, Napoleon swung his army east to confront the land armies of the Third Coalition.

This chapter addresses the organisation of the planned British defences in the years 1803 to 1805. It begins with an account of the different kinds of military personnel recruited to meet the invasion threat and prosecute the war, and the methods of recruitment and their impact upon civilian society. It then looks briefly at the physical defences commenced on the coast to impede any French landing, and the plans to drive into the country. It concludes with suggestions about what the organisation for invasion meant in the long term for British society.

Broadly speaking, and excluding the Royal Navy, there were three kinds of military force recruited in Britain during the wars: the regular army, the militia and various volunteer units. Throughout the eighteenth century it had been the policy of British governments to build up the regular army at the beginning of a war and to run it down immediately a peace was signed. The policy affected the system of internal defence during the years of the greatest invasion threats from Revolutionary and Napoleonic France. The rank and file of the regulars were volunteers, although sometimes the 'volunteering' was the result of trickery by a recruiting sergeant or recruiting agent. The behaviour of these agents, stigmatised as 'crimps', caused serious rioting in London in 1794, and again in 1795, when it was believed that young men had been kidnapped for army service. Some men were recruited from the courts by magistrates; serving the country was an alternative to a prison sentence, though the choice of either going to prison or going into the army was not necessarily offered to the offender. However, the regular army was also the strike force to be deployed in foreign fields – home defence relied, first and foremost, on the militia.

Every county had a militia regiment. In England militia organisation had a long tradition, but the system had been significantly reorganised and improved in 1757. The Irish militia had been allowed to lapse until the outbreak of war in 1793; the Scottish militia was a product of the war against Revolutionary France and was only formerly established in 1796–7.[2] In wartime the militia regiments were embodied to serve much like the regular army, except for the fact that militiamen could not be sent out of the kingdom without a special Act of Parliament. Each regiment was officered by members of the county gentry – the same social class that purchased rank in the regular army.

Theoretically the rank-and-file militiamen were recruited by ballot from all able-bodied men between the ages of eighteen and forty-five, but there were many exceptions to the ballot – poor men under five feet four inches or with at least one legitimate child, clergy, articled clerks, seamen, workmen in the royal arsenals and dockyards, and so forth. It was also possible, if balloted, for a man to pay a fine to avoid service or to hire a substitute. Insurance clubs grew up, into which men paid a small sum for the purpose of hiring a substitute or paying the fine. The problem was that once money was offered to men to act as substitutes, or to fill the gaps in the ranks for men who had paid the fine rather than serve, then the county militias were competing for men from the same pool as the regular army. There were stories of men taking one bounty, deserting and taking another. Shortly after the war recommenced in 1803 the *Leeds Intelligencer* reported that men in West Yorkshire, indulging in this form of trickery, were calling it, in a parody of their social superiors' former foreign visits, 'making the grand tour'.[3] In London such tricksters were called 'pair-makers': 'They have assumed the foregoing appellation, in allusion to their trade; for each person obtaining a bounty in the manner above described, is significantly said to have *made a pair*, and hence the labourer in that occupation is denominated a *pair-maker*.'[4] Such tricksters were a minority, but they excited considerable annoyance and concern.

It was not always apparent to young men looking for adventure whether a recruiting party was looking for men for the regular army or for substitutes for the militia. When plans were advanced for an overseas campaign it was common for the regular army to seek to fill its ranks by offering bounties to trained militiamen. In 1805, 13,580 men were recruited into the regular army from the militia, roughly 2,000 more than the army managed to recruit by other methods. Private Wheeler, one of the most celebrated chroniclers of Wellington's Peninsular campaign, joined the regular army from the militia.[5]

When the fear of invasion was at its height, the government tried to establish other forms of militia. In 1796 a Supplementary Militia and a Provisional Cavalry had been recruited. The former was raised once again when war recommenced in 1803, and the government also sought to ballot for an additional auxiliary force known as the Army of the Reserve. Like the militia, men who had been trained in the Army of the Reserve were encouraged to take a bounty and enlist with the regulars. Between 1803 and 1806 nearly 16,000 men did so, including another celebrated chronicler of the Peninsular War, Rifleman Harris.[6]

In Revolutionary France, and under Napoleon, the French met the demands for men with conscription. Napoleon's allies and some of his enemies also adopted different forms of conscription. The British resisted a formal policy of conscription, though the quotas of men required at different times from particular towns and counties, at various stages of the war, together with the ballots for the militia and similar bodies, came close to it. Moreover, the British succeeded in getting a very high percentage of their manpower under arms in the Royal Navy, the regular army and the militia. It is difficult to generalise about why men joined the British armed forces during the Revolutionary and Napoleonic period. Some were tricked, some were enlisted by violence. The latter appears to have been most usual when press gangs came ashore from warships determined to make up their complement. The professional recruiting officers in the seaports were usually keen to come to some sort of arrangement with the local authorities, since this kept relations cordial and reduced the chance of disorder.

Many recruits were motivated by patriotism. Stephen Morley wrote of the 'enthusiastic ardour in defence of their country' shown by young men in 1803. He enlisted in the Army of the Reserve and transferred to the regulars a year later.

Some were tempted by the bounties that were offered, especially if they or their families were in distress or if they were being bullied and beaten by a cruel master.[7] Others gave more personal reasons. In later life Joseph Mayett recalled enlisting in the Buckinghamshire Militia in terms that suggest youthful rebellion against his parents' religious convictions – convictions that he, himself, was subsequently to espouse: 'Satan was ready enough to tell me that religion was all a humm and that they which made such a fuss about it were a set of painted hypocrites altogether and I haveing the spirit of Cain my own Carnal nature sone Concured with the temtation and Satan obtained his ends.'[8]

In a third line of home defence, behind the regulars and the militia, there were the units of volunteer infantry and yeomanry cavalry, collectively known as 'volunteers'.[9] In the period 1803 to 1805 the numbers in these units hovered between 350,000 and 380,000. Patriotism was a great motivator here and historians have stressed the significance of volunteering, and participation in civic and national defence, in the moulding of ideas of being British, or belonging to a part of the nation.[10] However, the government's rash decision to exempt volunteers from militia ballots also made the corps especially attractive and it was not until some years after the invasion threat of 1803–5 that some rationality and formal structure was established for the auxiliary forces.

Generally the volunteer infantry were urban based and were recruited from all walks of life, including relatively poor men. Some men provided their own uniforms but the poorer volunteers were uniformed and equipped out of local subscriptions. Weapons were in short supply and in 1803 many volunteer infantry were issued with pikes. In March 1804 the postmaster of Chesterfield was expressing concerns about the fact that his town held 'near 150 Prisoners of War' but the four hundred volunteers in the town were without arms.[11] The yeomanry was generally recruited from men of a rather higher social standing than the urban infantry volunteers. Yeomanry cavalry ranged from the landed gentry, bringing their servants and tenants, to businessmen, tradesmen, independent farmers and their brothers and sons. The men were expected to come with their own horses, and to provide their own uniforms, arms and accoutrements.

Quite how the volunteers would have fared against the French must remain an open question. When the Irish Militia were pitted against General Humbert's veterans at Castlebar in 1798, they fled, even though they had numerical superiority. Arguably this feeble showing was the result of the militiamen being poorly equipped, and their morale appears to have been shaken and undermined by the Irish rebellion. In the previous year militiamen and yeomanry cavalry had formed a key component of the force that marched against General Tate's *Légion Noire* when it landed in Wales. But then Tate's unsavoury group of ex-convicts and desperadoes did not put up any resistance when they found the Welsh peasantry to be unwilling allies and a large military force against them.[12]

When, by mistake, the alarm was raised during the invasion scare of 1803–5, volunteers and yeomen assembled at their muster points. Early in 1804 the warning beacons were erroneously lit north of Newcastle and up to the Scottish border. The militia, yeomanry and volunteers were stood to arms. It was reported that in Kelso:

Within a few minutes after the alarm was given, the Roxburgshire Volunteers of the town district assembled, fully armed and accoutered [sic]; and, within half an hour, the centre troop of Yeomanry began to collect. It was extremely gratifying to observe the universal alacrity which pervaded every description of people upon that alarming occasion, many of the Volunteers, and the greater part of the Yeomanry, residing several miles from Kelso, some of them so far distant as 10 or 12 miles; yet, before 12 o'clock, that is, within two hours after the first alarm was given, almost every individual was assembled whose duty it was to be present at that rendezvous.[13]

There was a similar occurrence in West Yorkshire in the summer of 1805. On this occasion some furze had been set alight in line with the warning beacons and the local volunteers collected their arms and fell in for duty. The Yorkshire working men from the urban volunteer units involved were also careful to put in their claims for duty payment from the government.[14]

When called upon to act against native-born rioters, the volunteer forces proved formidable, though they could also be a risky weapon to rely upon. Yeomanry cavalry were commonly deployed against popular protest, since they were often the troops most readily available to the local civil power. However, a magistrate's request for yeomanry aid might also exacerbate a situation – if the trouble had erupted over the high price of foodstuffs and the belief that farmers were profiting, the deployment of farmers in yeoman regimentals to face down the crowd looked like partiality. On occasions during the serious food shortages shortly before the Peace of Amiens, members of urban volunteer infantry companies were reluctant to turn out to police their neighbours, while a few even participated in the disorders in uniform.[15]

There was a poor harvest in 1804, but the years of the greatest invasion threat did not experience the famine conditions and major disorders of 1795–6 and 1799–1801. Moreover, and this is a significant, if unsung, achievement, the commissariat appears to have ensured that the great military encampments in coastal districts (see Table 2) and the swollen ranks of seamen, ship's fitters and other workers in the naval ports, did not seriously disrupt local markets and create food shortages or high prices for the local communities. In consequence, the loyalty of volunteers and probably also that of some yeoman, was not tested as it might have been by demands for assistance from the civil power. However, there were examples of urban volunteers showing reluctance to be deployed against their neighbours.[16] The passage of a revised Corn Law through parliament in 1804 generated some disquiet and, as will be discussed below, there were recurrent concerns about attempts to subvert the soldiery. The volunteers often appeared the most vulnerable to subversion.[17]

Solidarity between members of a volunteer company could be stronger than acceptance of the necessities of war. In December 1803 the naval recruiting officers in Chester authorised a hot press. Local magistrates complained about the way in which the press gangs took farmers' servants travelling to market and broke open doors and seized tradesmen, freemen and apprentices, none of whom had ever been to sea. These men appear to have been released, but among

Table 2: Strength of Forces available to District Commanders in Britain, January to March 1804

District	Content	Regulars and Militia: effective rank and file	Volunteers and Yeomanry: effective rank and file
Southern	Kent, Surrey, Sussex (exclusive of London)	32,406	11,778
Eastern	Norfolk, Suffolk, Cambs, Hunts, Essex	28,720	21,561
London	(Including Surrey within the bills of mortality)	5,068	28,383
South-West	Hants, Wilts, Dorset	10,935	11,771
Western	Devon, Cornwall, Somerset (exclusive of Bristol, Bath, Troubridge, Uxbridge or other places garrisoned from Bristol)	9,518	26,043
North-Western	Cheshire, Salop, Lancs, North Wales	805	9,806
Northern	Northumberland, Cumberland, Westmoreland, Durham	5,466	14,126
Yorkshire	Yorkshire, Lincs	5,628	16,788
Isle of Wight		4,171	1,870
Severn	Glos, Worcs, Hereford, Monmouth, South Wales	1,542	7,945
Home	Middx, Herts, Berks	4,942	–
North Inland	Derbys, Notts, Staffs, Leics, Warwicks, Rutland	414	–
South Inland	Beds, Oxon, Bucks, Northants	Nil	–

Reserves of Volunteers additional to the above

Wakefield 14,303	Chester 2,200	Reading 6,566
Salisbury 5,042	Liverpool 3,287	Aylesbury 9,683
Bristol 8,495	Lichfield 29,140	Brentwood 10,738
Gloucester 12,451	Northampton 8,247	Dorking 7,299
	London 28,283	

Source: Fortescue, County Lieutenancies, Appendix XII, p 312.

those that the press held on to as an experienced seaman was Daniel Jackson, aged forty-six years and now a member of Chester's volunteer artillery company. After one of their normal parades on 28 December 1803 about a hundred of the Chester Volunteers marched on the Rendez Vous House to rescue Jackson. Major Joseph Wilmot remonstrated with his men and seized one of the ringleaders, but the man was promptly rescued by his comrades. Only after some two or three hours, and considerable persuasive efforts by the officers of the volunteers and the local magistrates, could the angry men be persuaded to return to their homes.[18]

The government was determined to make an example – it sought to organise a prosecution of the ringleaders of the trouble, but came up against a determination to prevent this happening from the local population, where, according to one correspondent, the volunteers included 'above one *fifth* of the males of all ages within this city'.[19] A man named Humphries, who had acted as a spokesman for the crowd, was eventually prosecuted and collapsed with an 'epileptic paroxysm' when the jury found him guilty. The city's magistrates signed a testimonial acknowledging his 'general good behaviour' and the Attorney General, who had led the prosecution, considered the offence 'much diminished' by the man's subsequent conduct.[20] The riot also became an issue in local politics when one of the volunteers, John Williamson, declared that his candidacy in elections for sheriff was to enable his fellow citizens to decide between the corps and its critics.[21] At least one other example of volunteers involved in resistance to a press gang was forwarded to the Home Office towards the end of the following year. In this instance it was the gang of a sloop put ashore in Cornwall – precisely the kind of naval-recruiting expedition most likely to create trouble.[22]

Turning out when the alarm was sounded was one thing; facing the fire of Napoleon's army could have been another. The solidarity shown among the men at Chester and elsewhere, even the local solidarity shown by some volunteers participating in food riots, might be taken as a good sign of a preparedness to stand up for the local community. Moreover, had they been deployed against French invaders, the volunteers would probably have considered themselves to be fighting for their own communities first and for the state second. It is possible also that a century of belief in the superiority of the Freeborn Englishman, or Briton, and the superiority of the British constitutional system, could have strengthened their determination against the French.

The first distinguished historians of the British response to the invasion threat wrote of a 'great terror',[23] yet many of the cartoons and caricatures of the period suggest a confidence that 'Boney's' head would be on a British pike in a matter of hours following his landing. Given the way that the French army sped to the Danube in 1805, then outmanoeuvred and trounced its opposition at Ulm and Austerlitz, such confidence could well have been misplaced. But then the reality is that the French invasion was never launched and the Grande Armée never poured over the beaches and into the countryside of south-east England. It remains the historian's task to explain what happened and while 'what if' may be a popular pastime among some historians, 'what if' remains pure (if sometimes money-spinning) speculation.

A final issue that needs to be considered with reference to the volunteers and the militia is the potential internal threat from British Jacobins. While there remains an unsettled debate as to the seriousness of this threat during the 1790s, there is no question that there were French sympathisers in the country, some of whom advocated revolutionary action and some of whom were prepared to join with a French invasion force.[24] According to one of the government's spies, John Moody – a shoe warehouseman who commonly signed his reports 'Notary' – the Chester disorder revived the spirits of extremists among London radicals. In January 1804 Moody wrote of radicals joining the volunteers to foment trouble.[25]

It was during the Peace of Amiens that a conspiracy had been detected in London, involving members of the brigade of guards and commanded by an Irish colonel who had been a comrade-in-arms of Admiral Nelson.[26] In September 1803 Humphrey Crawley had been sentenced to death at the Old Bailey for attempting to subvert a militia corporal.[27] But the scare was short lived – by mid-February 1804 Moody was reporting that very few were attending the meetings of the radical 'Middlesex committee'.[28] The concerns about radicals fomenting insurrection at home were never as pronounced after 1803 as they had been in the war against the French Revolution. A general disillusionment with Napoleon among many radicals is the probable reason for this – a disillusionment that was heightened by his decision to take an imperial crown in May 1804.[29]

Recruiting regular soldiers and auxiliaries to face a French landing was only part of the planning initiated to confront invasion. It was obvious that physical defences were also necessary to meet any French force that succeeded in crossing the Channel. The beaches of Kent and Sussex were the closest for the army encamped at Boulogne; it was also conceivable that a descent might be made on the Essex coast. From 1803 to 1805 there was nothing to impede the French on these beaches other than guns in earthen entrenchments. The various castles and garrisons along the coastline, notably Chatham and Dover, were significantly strengthened. A landing in Kent particularly, and a march on London to force the British to terms, would have required some form of assault upon or, at best, the containment of, these two strong points.

In 1803 discussions were begun about the construction of small, impregnable gun towers along the vulnerable coasts that might impede and inflict major damage on any invasion force. The model for these forts was a tower on Mortello Point, Corsica, that had used red-hot shot to beat off two British warships with considerable damage and heavy casualties in February 1794. The initial proposal for such towers on the coast was made in April 1798,[30] but the authorisation for surveying sites for the Martello towers – an English corruption of 'Mortello' – did not begin until the autumn of 1804. Construction did not start until the following spring and the seventy-three towers between Folkestone and Seaford were not completed until the end of 1806.[31] It was another year before twenty-nine larger towers were completed, running south from Aldeburgh in Suffolk.

At roughly the same time as the survey for the Martello towers, construction began on a second line of defence beyond the beaches of Kent and Sussex. This was a water barrier known as the Royal Military Canal. When completed the canal stretched from Shorncliffe to Cliff End; part of the route linked with the River

Rother. The canal was dug in a zigzag to facilitate artillery and musket fire directed at any force seeking to cross it. A military road ran on the north side to enable the rapid movement of men and materiel to wherever they might be needed. Like the towers, the canal was not completed until several years after the threat of 1803–5.[32]

In addition to confronting the French by force of arms, and impeding any invasion with strong points and barriers, consideration was also given to depriving the enemy of local food and draft animals. In 1779, during the American War of Independence, there had been some anxiety about a French landing, and plans had been mooted to drive the country. The plans were revived in 1801 and 1803 – on both occasions the Duke of Richmond, Lord Lieutenant of Sussex, a one-time Master General of the Ordnance, was highly critical: he queried whether such action was possible. Moreover, no doubt mindful of the famine brought about by the poor harvests of the 1790s, he wondered whether it was desirable, fearing that the destruction of food supplies could lead to starvation among those unable to get away from the French.[33]

Richmond's concerns appear to have given the government pause, but some instructions were still sent out to the counties and were acted upon. Parochial officers were required to appoint individuals within their local communities respectively to remove all horses and wagons, cattle, sheep and other livestock, as well as all grain and 'dead-stock'. At the same time bakers were required to sign undertakings that they would supply specific amounts of bread for British troops in the event of invasion.[34]

As with the question of how militiamen and volunteers would have stood up to French artillery and musketry, it is impossible to answer the question as to how the various defence plans would have fared in the event of invasion. When the threat was at its height, neither the Martello Towers nor the Royal Military Canal had been completed. However, earthworks and effective artillery fire and musketry could have proved devastating, even to a very large force of possibly sea-sick troops struggling to get ashore with wet arms and powder. It seems likely that there would have been confusion, at least in some quarters, over whether or not to try to drive the country. Such a policy, even if only partly attempted, could have led to clogged roads that would have impeded both French invaders and British defence forces. Reinforced strong points such as Chatham and Dover would have presented serious threats to French supply lines. Yet it is also the case that a major victory, followed by a determined push on to London, might have secured a British surrender.

It has to be admitted that the British government's recruitment policies during the Revolutionary and Napoleonic Wars were not always well considered and that sometimes they acted against each other. The recruiting and equipping of large numbers of regulars and militia had a significant effect on some areas of the economy, while the deployment of large numbers of troops on the coasts was not always popular with the local communities. Troops, generally young men, with nothing much to do other than wait for the French, occasionally got drunk, fought each other, poached and indulged in a bit of vandalism or pillage. The improvements to existing defences and the building of new ones brought some work to local communities, though the new defences were not available when the threat of invasion was at its height. Knowing when the threat was at its height, however, is one of the benefits of hindsight available to historians – not to the politicians and military planners of the time.

The victory at Trafalgar effectively destroyed the threat of invasion, but the war was to continue for another decade, and, as the coastal defences were enlarged and strengthened, so did the government also bring a greater degree of rationality to the structure and organisation of the auxiliary forces for home defence. In particular the Local Militia, established in 1808, increasingly eclipsed the volunteers and gave much more effective training and greater uniformity to the auxiliaries.

It is difficult to provide precise figures but it seems fair to conclude that, towards the end of the first decade of the nineteenth century, Britain was supporting a regular armed force of roughly one man in every nine or ten of its population of military age – setting military age at eighteen to forty-five, the years during which a man was liable for the militia ballot. If the volunteers and Local Militia are fed into the equation, the number rises to one man in every five or six.[35] Some areas of the nation contributed more than others: Scotland and Ireland, for example, sent more of their young men into the army and navy than did England; and the coastal counties sent more men into the sea service. While it may have varied from place to place and region to region, the overall scale of the effort was enormous. It is inconceivable that it left no legacy, though pinning down the precise nature of that legacy is not straightforward.

The Revolutionary and Napoleonic Wars were the first to be written up by ordinary participants in Britain in any numbers; there are well over one hundred memoirs of the Peninsular War alone.[36] This suggests a confidence among veterans, most of whom had served in the ranks, or on the lower decks, that they had stories worth telling. It suggests also that there was an audience keen to read these stories. The auxiliaries who did not transfer into the regular army, did not write up their memoirs in the same way. But this did not diminish their participation or the experience and memory of that participation.

Urban elites appear to have looked at their volunteer companies with feelings of civic pride: these companies gave them an opportunity to assert their own importance and independence from the traditional county elites. For the poorer man, his service emphasised his personal significance to the local community and to the state. This was something that radicals were to pick up on in their calls for the vote.[37] Hanoverian Britain perceived itself as a Protestant isle protected by Providence, but Catholics were called upon as never before in the struggle against Napoleon, and, as participation gave ammunition to the case for political reform, so did it also strengthen the case for Catholic emancipation.

The ordinary men who stood on the decks of wooden walls, and those who stood behind them on the coasts waiting for the French invasion had a mixture of motives ranging from patriotism – both national and local – to varying degrees of self-interest. It would be wrong to think of them coming forward to serve purely for what they might get out of it – but it would also be wrong to assume that, to a man, they did not expect any change to come as a result of their participation. It would be equally wrong to assume that participation in itself did not contribute to a reshaping of their aspirations for future developments.

La Grande Armée of 1805

From the Great Ocean to the Great Continent

MICHAEL BROERS

Historical tropes are often written off as clichés, but the long wars between Britain and France between the years 1793 and 1815 show that, in this case at least, the recurring conflicts between commercial, maritime societies governed by open institutions and more authoritarian, militaristic land powers were an intrinsic part of European history. Contemporary politicians, naval and military commanders were all men rooted in their Classical educations, and the continuum – as quite distinct from abstract comparisons – with Sparta and Athens, and even more with Rome and Carthage – were at the forefront of their minds.

By his own lights, Napoleon was forging a new order in France in the years between the Battle of Marengo in 1800 and Trafalgar, consciously predicated on late republican and early imperial Rome; his nomenclature, but above all the civil institutions he shaped, found their models, as well as their inspiration, in Roman precedents. He set about restoring order after the long and bloody republican civil war of the 1790s, an integral part of which involved consolidating French hegemony over western and south-western Europe, which, in turn, entailed rebuilding the army in his own image. Britain responded to this by turning in on itself, emphasising its traditions of individualism, taking pride in the civilising virtues of its seaborne commerce and material prosperity, of vaunting itself as a nation of polite, commercial and, above all else, free people.[1] The twin outcomes of this rivalry were the battles of Trafalgar and Austerlitz.

In more down-to-earth terms, these wars – and the fighting of 1805, more than any other moment – are a retelling of the quarrel between the elephant and the whale, made historical reality. This chapter tells the tale from the elephant's point of view, as it were. Any full examination of the significance of the Battle of Trafalgar should encompass the nature and magnitude of the threat Britain faced from across the Channel in the years between the collapse of the Peace of Amiens in 1802, and the moment when, chastened in some part by the obliteration of his fleet by Nelson, Napoleon abandoned the invasion of England, and turned against the land armies of the Third Coalition. At no other time were the different, but equally powerful, fighting qualities of the Napoleonic elephant and the Nelsonian whale more on display, than in the great 'stand off' of 1802–5.

Napoleon was not idle in these years, however unrealistic his hopes of crossing the Channel eventually proved. While his attempts to control the sea routes came undone, simultaneously, Napoleon was able to forge a new army in the Channel ports, the likes of which Europe had never seen. The Grande Armée was the most fearsome war machine of its age, with the sole and ultimately decisive exception of the Royal Navy. The evolution of the Grande Armée needs to be explored on three distinct levels. The first concerns the diplomatic and military developments of these unnaturally quiet years, operating on a geopolitical level, for these gave rise to the conditions that created the Grande Armée, and then changed its role. Alongside this wider picture are the internal reforms within Napoleonic France between 1799 and 1805, which made the forging of the Grande Armée possible. Finally, at the heart of the process, was the particular experience of the Camp de Boulogne, which gave the Grande Armée its enduring character.

War and Diplomacy

The process that led to the emergence of the Grande Armée, perversely, began with the Peace of Amiens in 1802, and ended with the definitive British naval victory of Trafalgar. The period of general peace in Europe, between 1800 and 1805, bought all the powers vital breathing space in a war that had begun as early as 1792 for the main protagonists, Revolutionary France and the Habsburg Monarchy. The war that was rekindled between Britain and France would prove decisive to the evolution of Napoleon's ambitions, but it is equally important to remember that, between 1802 and 1805, it was of a very limited nature, fought largely at sea and in the colonies – and did not involve any of France's major military rivals. This afforded Napoleon the chance to regroup and reform, and he took it: the Grande Armée was, paradoxically, the product of a period of peace.

These years saw French overseas ambitions either willingly abandoned – as through the Louisiana Purchase – or simply thwarted by British naval superiority. As a result, the invasion of Britain should be seen as the last phase – the last desperate gamble – of the Anglo-French imperial struggle of the eighteenth century. When it failed, France was ready – almost in spite of herself – to turn east and south, towards Europe. If the protracted period of peace on the continent between 1800 and 1805 bought all the great powers time, only Napoleon and the British actually made good use of it.

However, these judgements come very much with the benefit of hindsight. There can be little serious doubt that Napoleon took the invasion of Britain seriously, and in the context of the times, it might have proved a costly diversion from more pressing threats. Between June 1803 and June 1805, he concentrated over 50 per cent of all his effective troops in the Channel ports. This amounted to over 190,000 men and 340 pieces of artillery. The seriousness of his intent is really grasped when the internal condition of France in these years is brought to mind.

The Reform of France

These years saw the two great adversaries, Britain and France, gear themselves up for long-term hostilities, albeit in utterly different ways. Napoleon used this period to reform the administration of France, to create the Gendarmerie, the prefectoral corps, and institute the mechanisms and the professional personnel needed for mass conscription on a regular basis. The civilian administrators, who would enforce conscription and maintain order in the provinces, were to be trained in the new *lycées* and the refounded University, just as his new officers would emerge from the reformed military academies of St Cyr and Fontainebleau. France was a reforged country, not just a reforged army, by 1805.

Napoleon did not inherit a peaceful country, or one that was well disposed to his regime. It is all too easily forgotten that Napoleon was brought to power not just to turn the tide of the war, which was running badly against France when he became First Consul, late in 1799. He was also there to put down civil war, counter-revolution and general rural disorder, consisting mainly of brigandage and peasant revolts against taxation and conscription.

One of the major constraints on the development of a large, well-trained cavalry arm in the Channel ports was that no less than twenty-four squadrons of dragoons were needed for service in these years, fighting the royalist peasant rebellions in western France.[2] Indeed, murder, revolt and a breakdown of central government were almost the norm in large tracts of southern and western France; in Brittany and western Normandy, the royalist peasant guerrillas – the *Chouans*, or 'sparrowhawks', named for the bird-call imitations they used as signals – were always waiting for a British naval landing.

Napoleon dealt with all this in a ruthless, remarkably effective fashion. His campaigns of 'internal pacification' are a hallmark of his rule in his first years at the helm of France, but they were achieved without his best troops. The seminal research of Howard Brown into the pacification of France in the period immediately before and after Napoleon's seizure of power in late 1799 has shown, among many other things, that garrison life for those troops not in the Channel ports was anything but the dull, inactive existence that more traditional military histories have claimed.[3] Desertion was, indeed, rife in many units in southern France – because life there was dangerous, not because it was dull.[4]

The line regiments and dragoons posted to the troubled regions of southern and western France may not have taken part in the formative experience of the main army between 1802 and 1805, but nor did they undergo anything like an ossifying peacetime experience. Whereas their comrades were being trained and kept busy in the Camp de Boulogne and its satellites, the men of the Army of the Interior received a hardening, embittering education in civilian guerrilla war, and learned for and by themselves, a particularly ruthless, increasingly structured approach to counter-insurgency. They would have need of this when confronted by ferocious peasant revolts in Italy, the Tyrol and, above all, in Spain, in the years of imperial expansion that followed Austerlitz.

In the convulsed circumstances of provincial France in the first years of Napoleonic rule, it is arguable that they had the most difficult posting of any branch of the service. Initially, they stood in the frontline of the counter-insurgency efforts against royalist rebellions, political in-fighting left over from the Revolutionary upheavals of the 1790s, and common brigandage. As will be seen, this was only the beginning: their next, and continuing, task would be the enforcement of conscription.

Brown's meticulous archival research in provincial France has shown how widespread and serious violent disorder was in the early years of Napoelonic rule. Over much of rural France, open revolt, the robbing of mail coaches, the seizure of the municipal strong boxes containing tax receipts and the murder of local government officials were all too common. Even in this unsettled context, Napoloen was still prepared to divert most of his troops – and his best troops, at that – to the new 'Army of the Ocean Coasts'. He requested 1,500 men be drawn from each line regiment to create it.[5] That is how much the invasion of England obviously meant to him. He had to build his new army at the height of the process of pacification and to refashion the French state to meet his military needs, and those needs were gargantuan.

The implacable, if shoestring, process of counter-insurgency was largely successful by the outbreak of the War of the Third Coalition in 1805, and the particular fruit it would bear for the Grande Armée was the ability to enforce mass conscription on the French countryside. In the immediate context of the years 1802–5, however, the projected invasion of Britain denuded the forces on the ground of their best effectives during the crucial period of the restoration of order. In this context, the achievement of the members of the Military Commissions who oversaw this process, and the often brutal soldiers they directed, emerges as truly remarkable, however ruthless.

Napoleon's more immediate achievements in rebuilding France took place at the centre and the apex of the state. He accomplished, by careful research and administrative management, what Robespierre had sought to do through the bloody purges during the notorious Terror period of 1793–4, especially that of the Hébertistes, a political faction particularly embroiled in the War Ministry. A crucial reason for the radicalisation of revolutionary politics in these years had been the notorious corruption of the Ministry of War and the way this hampered the war effort. Napoleon found and discarded the same men Robespierre had railed at – henceforth, his troops could count on a relatively honest and efficient civilian administration.

In 1802 he created a separate War Administration Office from the older, deeply corrupt Ministry of War. In the period when the invasion of Britain was his major priority, he entrusted the new department to none other than his closest military collaborator, Berthier, the trusty Chief of Staff known to the troops as 'Napoleon's wife'.[6] Napoleon had first-hand experience of the corruption in the military administration, and he knew it spread from top to bottom. As recently as the Second Italian campaign of 1800–1, he had seen his troops deprived of supplies and munitions by corrupt *fournisseurs* – official suppliers – and the lowest rung on the administrative ladder, the *commissaires de guerres*, when he was actually the head of the French state.

These problems were never entirely overcome; the Grande Armée was never properly paid and only rarely well supplied, and then only on foreign soil when it saw to its own needs directly. Nevertheless, by 1803, Napoleon had made tangible progress, as was evident in the 1805 campaign. He thoroughly purged the army administration and many of the worst offenders were sent to the 'dry guillotine' of Saint Domingue – modern-day Haiti – between 1801 and 1803. It was easier to get a grip on corruption in peacetime than in war, and these years were Napoleon's only real chance to do so until the relative lull of 1810–11; even in 1805, he found it easier to levy taxes on enemy Austrian territory and draw contributions from the allied states of southern Germany, than to put too much strain – or faith – in the bureaucracy.[7]

Napoleon brought many of the basic reforms of the earlier revolutionaries to bear on his most important work, the creation of a regular system of universal conscription. The Directory, the regime that preceded Napoleon, had already created the basis of the conscription system in the 'Jourdan Law' of 1798, named after the general who drew it up, but Napoleon's reforms gave it life. In 1790 the revolutionary government had created the *État Civil*, whereby all births, deaths and marriages had to be registered with the civil authorities, no longer with the Church, to be legalised.

Napoleon was now able to use these registers to gain at least a general idea of the male population of conscription age in France. This meant he could assign realistic quotas of conscripts to each of the administrative units the revolution had also created in 1790 – the departments which were much easier to control than the large, anachronistic provinces of the old monarchy. The prefects, centrally appointed civil servants accountable directly to Napoleon and his Minister of the Interior, were put in charge of each department, a Napoleonic innovation that replaced the elected councils of the Revolutionary period. They knew from the outset that the enforcement of conscription was their main task, and they toured their departments at least three times a year – at each levy – visiting even the smallest towns and villages, to oversee the process of drawing lots and assuring the compliance of all those eligible.[8]

The convulsed circumstances of much of rural France in these years show that this was far from an easy task. Conscripting the French peasant – most conscripts, like most Frenchmen, were peasants – was far from a paper exercise. The efficient Napoleonic bureaucracy, and the meticulous records it has left historians, should not hide the grim, often brutal reality of what became known to contemporary French people as 'the blood tax'. Indeed, the first major revolt against the new Revolutionary government came not when Louis XVI was overthrown in August 1792, nor even when he was guillotined a few months later. Rather, the first great uprising came in the spring of 1793, in the remote Vendée region of western France, when, in desperation, faced with an advancing Prussian army, the government sought to impose a 'mass levy'.

They were still fighting Napoleon in 1803, and even he was finally forced to give this region an artificially light conscription quota. The real 'teeth' of the conscription system became the Gendarmerie, a paramilitary police force Napoleon inherited from the Directory, but which he rejuvenated, turning it into a fearsome and, by the standards of the time, an unprecedented military presence, disseminated all over the French countryside. Many French veterans of the 1790s were demobilised after the Treaties of Campo Formio and Amiens and soon found employment in its ranks.[9]

The Gendarmerie was actually under the command of the Ministry of War, and was part of the regular army, although the prefects usually commanded its forces during conscription levies, and could always call on them to restore order locally. Gendarmes were drawn from the army; they were usually non-commissioned officers, who had served in at least three campaigns with distinction, and had clean disciplinary records. The corps was also officially required to be six feet tall or above and have basic literacy skills, but these requirements were not always met in practice. Gendarmes were spread in six-man brigades through the countryside, placed in permanent barracks in the smallest towns; most men came from outside the regions in which they served. Nothing like this had ever happened before; henceforth, rebellious peasants had to confront a permanent military force in their midst. Above all, it meant that conscription was going to be enforced to the full. It was the Gendarmerie, through the sheer persistence that this permanent, localised presence afforded it, which gradually wore down peasant resistance to conscription.

This whole system, taken together, guaranteed Napoleon regular levies of conscripts on a massive scale. Even after the catastrophe of the 1812 campaign in Russia, when, at a conservative estimate, he lost 380,000 men, the now well-honed machinery of conscription, embracing as it did the whole edifice of local government and policing, ensured that Napoleon had over 100,000 new recruits in the depots on his bedraggled return. For the first time, France, the most populous state in Europe, had harnessed its manpower efficiently. Indeed, with the absorbtion of modern Belgium in 1795, of Germany west of the Rhine in 1797, and of much of northern Italy in 1802, Napoleon's reserves of men grew higher still. He would need them.

Neither the lightning victories of the Second Italian campaign of 1800–1, nor the far more important successes of Moreau in the main theatres of Switzerland and southern Germany, could hide the hard truth from Napoleon that he had inherited a shambles of an army from the Directory in 1799. His whole strategy in 1800 had been geared to a quick victory and a comprehensive peace settlement, because he knew, from his unique vantage point as both head of state and commander-in-chief, that France could not sustain a protracted conflict. The army's command structures were disparate and disjointed, the product of the desperate, ad hoc expedients of almost ten years of war, for which the Revolutionary governments had been ill prepared.

Although the officer corps, especially its higher echelons, were notable for their youth, the core of the ranks was ageing, its NCOs in particular, many of whom were soon destined to swell the ranks of the Gendarmerie. It was also appallingly trained. Napoleon and Moreau, who was really the leading commander of the late 1790s, had already begun their own reforms within their respective armies, even during the course of the 1800–1 hostilities, so serious were the problems they perceived. They organised their armies into corps during these campaigns, thus expanding the concept of self-contained divisions that had emerged under the Directory. However, Napoleon also diluted the concept of the corps as a wholly sufficient unit by concentrating his cavalry into a separate reserve corps – this would influence later developments at the Channel ports in 1803–5, and Imperial army corps tended to consist mainly of infantry and artillery, with only light cavalry in support for reconnaissance and skirmishing duties.

At subordinate levels, little was ever done to alter the basic units, created by the Revolution, of brigades and demi-brigades.[10] More important was the lack of basic training in the army; Napoleon had infantry units doing basic parade-ground drills and target practice during the fighting in 1800. In the period of the Peace of Amiens, he had already instituted the regular drills and parades – three times every ten days – that would characterise routine in the Channel camps. For troops based around Paris, and even for those in transit, Napoleon took personal charge of drill as often as possible.[11]

As early as 1801, Napoleon appointed Marmont Inspector-General of Artillery, with a brief to root out useless practices, standardise and raise the level of expertise, introduce new weaponry and familiarise the troops with it. This took time and much of Marmont's work was cut short by the outbreak of war in 1805, but real progress was made, even before the creation of the Channel camps.[12] When war resumed with Britain in 1803, Napoleon had already identified the army's problems and began the process of dealing with them. When this was coupled with the increasing success of the internal pacification of rural France, it also meant he could now be assured of the workings of conscription, and therefore of fresh and plentiful recruits to replace the veterans of the 1790s.

The Camp of Boulogne

All of this was brought to bear during the creation of the Grande Armée in the Channel ports in 1803–5. The Revolutionary armies were all but spent as a force in 1799, and Napoleon knew it. The bulk of the troops assembled to invade Britain were new conscripts, usually reluctant peasants, not the ideological zealots of the 1790s. Thus, by 1805, a wholly new army had been created and unleashed on Europe, when its path to Britain was checked. The proposed invasion of England provided a heaven-sent opportunity to forge a new kind of army from the mass of new recruits, and it is this circumstance that gives history the evolution of the 'Army of the Ocean Coasts' of 1803 into the Grande Armée of 1805. This is what really lends these years their long-term significance in the story of the Napoleonic wars: a very new, powerful elephant was born in the barracks of the Channel ports. This period marked the creation of the most formidable army in the history of Europe up to that time.

In June 1803 the fragile peace between Britain and France finally collapsed. Napoleon's immediate reply was to shift the bulk of his troops to the Channel ports, and begin the construction of an artificial harbour at Boulogne, from which he hoped to embark his troops' transports for the invasion of England; he chose almost the same site as Caesar, for his invasion in 55 BC.[13] Camp would not formally be broken until 29 June 1805. Five more major camps soon followed that at Boulgone along the coast: Brest, Montreuil, St Omer, Bruges and Utrecht; each one was the headquarters of an army corps.

It was in these conditions that Napoleon consolidated the corps system and made it the pivot for the Grande Armée's structures. In the Channel ports, the Army of the Ocean Coasts was organised into seven more or less self-contained units of 20,000 men each, under his best generals: Soult, Ney, Davout, Marmont, Augereau, Bernadotte and Lannes, who would all distinguish themselves in the campaigns of the following years. Each corps had artillery, light cavalry and logistical units, as well as its main component of infantry, enabling them to fight as free-standing units if required. In addition to the corps, Napoleon brought Murat to the ports with a separate cavalry corps.

What really mattered, however, was what Napoleon now did with them. This period could have been disastrous for the Army of the Ocean Coasts; the bordeom of garrison life might have led to sloth, poor morale and even poorer effectiveness, in stark contrast to the pressures of the counter-insurgency in the western and southern departments. Instead, Napoleon instituted the regular drills he had hitherto only been able to impose on troops under his direct command – even forcing the whole army to learn how to swim, in anticipation of amphibious landings. This raised fitness levels to almost unheard-of heights, just as the drills for embarking and landing from the flimsy troop transports instilled great precision at platoon level: 67,500 men were able to embark and disembark in a quarter of an hour.

Napoleon held full parades, under his own inspection, three times every ten days. Veteran NCOs trained the new recruits in their own way, without a great deal of uniformity, but train them they did. The young officers, recently graduated from the new military academies, learned from them, too. For the first time, the army was properly paid and uniformed, as well as fed and quartered. This proved a rare occurrence in the history of the Grande Armée, but the drill and the discipline were now a habit, and would remain so.

Boulogne was of particular importance for Murat's work with the cavalry: horsemen took a very long time to train, and the French cavalry had never been an effective force until this point. The cavalry emerged from the Channel camps as a virtual weapon of mass destruction, its heavy units able to smash massed infantry on the battlefield, while the light cavalry were used in deadly pursuit of broken, retreating formations afterwards. The mounted corps learned how to ford rivers and still keep formation, while the dragoons also did full infantry drills. Without the time and concentration the 'wait' to invade England gave him, Murat would have found it very difficult to achieve this transformation on the scale he did.

This whole process may have been the fortuitous result of diplomacy and the fact that during these years France had only one enemy and only one realistic hope of defeating it – a seaborne invasion. Nevertheless, the state of the military machine Napoleon had inherited in 1799 made it wholly necessary. The army that went into the camps as the Consular Army of the Ocean Coasts, and emerged over two years later as the Imperial Grande Armée, was, in the main, a new animal. The purges and retirements Napoleon effected after the Second Italian campaign meant that only one third of the army had more than six years' service, although well over 50 per cent had seen some combat.

It has been estimated that as few as one in thirty of the ranks were 'white coats' from the old royal army.[14] There was probably a fair proportion of 'blues' in the camps, volunteers of the 1792–4 period, imbued with the republican values of those years. However, the bulk of the army were conscripts from the first levy organised under the Jourdan Law of 1798; increasingly, they were joined by new recruits without any combat experience. Whether from years of self-reliance that bred too much independence, or from sheer rawness, the troops in the Channel ports needed exactly what Napoleon ensured they got: basic training with no nonsense, discipline on the parade ground and the most intangible element of all, *esprit du corps*. The whole process brought new recruits, hardened veterans and young officers together; the men and their officers came to know each other. They all now knew their commander, Napoleon himself, above all.

This work did not stay confined to the Channel camps. During these years, Napoleon created the military college at Fontainebleau, both for new boys taken from civilian life, and to instil theoretical training in the youthful veterans. Beside Fontainebleau – which by no coincidence was Napoleon's favourite official residence – he created a cavalry school in the great stables of Versailles, to which every cavalry regiment in the army sent one officer and one NCO for training.[15] Such levels of training did not extend to the whole of the Grande Armée by any means. Any literate soldiers and lower-ranking officers – and they were few and far between – were quickly seconded to administrative duties. Even many regimental colonels knew little French, and they were usually brutal men, but they were energetic, dutiful and all proven war leaders.

Most of the corps commanders – made Marshals on the creation of the Empire – had little formal training themselves. There were two striking exceptions to this, however. Davout and Soult emerged in these years as strict disciplinarians, and the latter trained his men very intensely; at Ostend, Davout concentrated more on overseeing his officers and conducted major manoeuvres through them every two weeks. Both Marshals enforced military discipline at all times. Ney was more typical, however; he spent a great deal of time on target practice and combat training, but did very little drilling, despite Napoleon's direct orders.[16]

All this, good and bad, was imparted to the men under their command. Discipline did not extend far beyond the parade ground, nor did *esprit du corps* reach much beyond exactly that – the corps. Violent rivalries between corps were notorious, as was duelling among the officers. The enmity between the cavalry and the artillery has been described by its finest historian as little short of hatred.[17] In these conditions, Napoleon was already emerging as the only real, unifying focus of loyalty. The arrival of raw, extremely reluctant peasant conscripts alongside the die-hard republican 'blues' of the 1790s, the juxtaposition of young cadet officers and hardened veteran NCOs, with wilful, egotistical commanders above them, lent itself to only one solution – the personalisation of power, authority and, above all, loyalty in the person of Napoleon. In this regard, for all the eccentricities attendant on the corps system, the Grande Armée was truly Napoleon's creation. It was far from perfect, but nothing comparable to it in power, effectiveness or spirit had ever been seen on land before in Europe.

Napoleon incarnated his military ideal in one unit, and he set it before the rest of the Grande Armée as the living embodiment of what it was supposed to be. In 1804, Napoleon moved his elite corps, the Imperial Guard, to Boulogne, under his personal command. The Guard was the cream of the army, highly trained, its members drawn only from the most distinguished veterans. Its presence helped to raise standards and aspirations among the rest of the troops, although admiration and emulation were already mixed with a justifiable resentment among the line regiments of the Guard's many privileges.[18] Indeed, when the Grande Armée broke camp for the 1805 campaign, Napoleon granted the Guard an extra pair of boots per man[19] – this not withstanding the fact that it went to war in ox-drawn carts, not on foot. By the end of the campaign, most line regiments could only reshoe themselves by seizing local supplies in Germany, the quartermaster's stores at Boulogne having proved inadequate from the outset.[20]

For all this, the Guard set a standard others were compelled to match – its discipline and courage were there for all to see, for the first time at Boulogne. Those who entered it did so after distinguished active service in the line regiments; its privileges were hard-earned. In all this, the Guard symbolised and encapsulated a very new kind of army. Late in 1805, in appalling weather and at the wrong time of year, according to convention, the Grande Armée was set loose – and the Guard set the pace – for a campaign no contemporary could possibly have envisaged.

Austerlitz

The proof of the success of the experience of the Channel camps came on the heels of the disaster of Trafalgar and Napoleon's abandonment of the invasion project. Britain's continental allies, Austria and Russia, took the field in the summer of 1805 on the assumption that it would take Napoleon months to get his army from the coast into central Europe. They were wrong, and their assumption was a clear sign that no one in the Allied camp had any clear idea what Napoleon had fashioned. The fitness and discipline instilled in the troops saw them reach the Danube in the unprecedented time of four weeks, marching at a measured pace, with a five-minute halt each hour.

The Imperial Guard got there in just over a fortnight. When they arrived, they were still fit to give battle. The whole operation took place in great secrecy, as orders were passed down the chain of command seamlessly and executed smoothly. The clearest sign of the high level of morale within the Grande Armée was the very low number of desertions it suffered en route: Davout and Soult's corps – a combined total of almost 40,000 men – lost less than forty. All this, it should be noted, took place in late autumn, often in rain and snow. It culminated in the crushing Napoleonic victory over a combined Austro-Russian army at Austerlitz, on 2 December 1805.

The Grande Armée would go on to other resounding victories, but none rivalled Austerlitz. It would never have the same levels of health or fitness again, as the wars dragged on and new recruits increasingly had to both learn on the job and live off the land. By 1807, the Napoleonic soldier was badly uniformed, indifferently armed, intermittently paid, fed by chance and led by grasping generals. However, for one shining moment in 1805, all the best elements of military life had been brought together, and Napoleon could draw on it, until the end.

Austerlitz and Trafalgar

It is easy with hindsight to see that Napoleon's invasion plans were futile. As will be explored in depth elsewhere in this volume, it is clear that the landing and transport craft designed at Boulogne had no real chance of success in crossing the Channel, even without an attack from the British fleet. The elephant was more land-locked than any dared to imagine. Yet, in the wake of Austerlitz, contemporaries can be forgiven for feeling no sense of complacency if they were British, or despondency, if French. Trafalgar was the truly defining battle of the two, but in the last days of 1805 and for many years thereafter, it did not look that way to many.

French military superiority went on being confirmed until 1812, and the war elephant fought on with exceptional persistence for some time thereafter. The British could celebrate Trafalgar, but not relax. If an examination of the character, strengths and even weaknesses of the Grande Armée reveals anything about the heat of the moment in 1805, it is the unheralded power and potential for destruction it could have reaped in Britain had, somehow, even one corps from it crossed the Channel. Hindsight has its uses, but so does the imagination to look into contemporary preoccupations.

In the short term, both societies, as much as both governments, took from these two battles the messages they most wanted to hear. Both had triumphed, both had foundered, both emerged stronger to fight each other another day with renewed confidence. 1805 was a very odd year in the history of the Napoleonic Wars. It was triumph mixed with tragedy, strategic defeat disguised by stunning tactical victory. The struggle between Britain and France in the Napoleonic Wars was mirrored on a personal level in the duel between Nelson and Napoleon, and both were victims of their moments of triumph. Nelson died at Trafalgar, yet his efforts stemmed the French tide; Napoleon's greatest military victory at Austerlitz – which is quite something in so remarkable a career – came as the result of the frustration engendered by Trafalgar, when he had to abandon the invasion of Britain, and it did nothing to solve the underlying problem of British resistance.

Yet, following the news of Austerlitz, the Younger Pitt ordered the map of Europe rolled up, as it would not be needed for some time. A new stage in the conflict had been reached, and the Grande Armée had now emerged the equal, but not the counterpart, of the Royal Navy. The whale and the elephant had their respective moments of glory in late 1805. It was no coincidence that they reached their peaks of power and fighting prowess well away from each other.

– 8 –

Austerlitz and the French

PETER HICKS

IN AUGUST 1805, NAPOLEON, with his eyes apparently fixed on invasion of the British Isles, performed a strategic pirouette and drove an army of seven divisions faster than any army had ever been driven before, to achieve (arguably) France's greatest ever military victory, Austerlitz. A whole army was captured at Ulm without a blow struck, the city of Vienna was taken for the first time ever in her history, here again without a shot fired. And finally an Allied army commanded by two emperors was outgunned, diplomatically, strategically and tactically – all by a Corsican upstart.

Such a great victory was naturally the stimulus for many French monuments during the First Empire, and throughout the nineteenth century it remained a symbol of Napoleonic, Bonapartist and French grandeur. Today, however, few in France know the significance of these monuments or the meaning of the battle. Indeed, despite the battle's importance, the 200th anniversary was largely ignored by the French government – a striking contrast to the Nelson and Trafalgar commemorations in Britain.

This article is tripartite, beginning with a consideration of the diplomatic run-up to the battle, continuing with a review of the battle's afterlife and ending with a reflection on the French government's inability to grasp the Napoleonic nettle.[1]

International Relations

In the spring and summer of 1805 the climate in European international relations was deteriorating rapidly; in May and June, two linked events occurred that were to lead directly to the conflict at Austerlitz. First, Napoleon completed his project to become the 'New Charlemagne' and had himself crowned 'King of Italy'. Secondly, he annexed the strategically important northern Italian region of Liguria (with its significant port of Genoa) to the Empire. Whilst these two events sent shockwaves throughout diplomatic Europe, they particularly worried Britain, Russia and Austria.

The fact is that Napoleon's actions had disrupted the traditional aims that these countries pursued under normal circumstances – what you could call their default foreign-policy positions. One of Russia's primary aims in international relations, for example, was the ability to act freely in the Mediterranean, therefore French control of the port of Genoa was particularly annoying. For Britain, the prime policy mover was the freedom to trade; here again, the closing of the port of Genoa to British shipping was a thorn in the side. Britain and France had been at 'phoney' war with each other since the collapse of the Peace of Amiens (in 1803), with France massing troops on her northern coasts with clear intentions to attempt a crossing.

As regards Austria, she traditionally had territorial expectations in north and north-eastern Italy, namely in Friuli, Istria, and the region around Venice. Napoleon as 'King of Italy' put an end to all that. In addition to these desires, the different countries of Europe also had various fundamental dislikes. Austria was wary of Russia and resisted at all costs Russia's encroachment, particularly in sensitive areas such as Silesia; Russia did not want Prussia in Poland; Prussia always tended towards expansion and found French occupation of the left bank of the Rhine a constriction.

Behind these conflicting policies stood the two fundamentally different geopolitical viewpoints of the superpowers of the day, Britain and France. Britain aimed at control of the seas to achieve a dominant position; France aimed at domination of mainland Europe in order to achieve her premier position. As for its policy towards the continent, Britain's aim was to maintain it as an area of small and medium powers, all vying against each other and so preventing the emergence of a possible rival to her imperial designs. As for her maritime designs, France tried at all costs to contest British control over world maritime trade and attempted parallel imperial conquests.

The Explosion of 1805

What lit the (already smouldering) fuse in 1805 was British attempts to escape the stranglehold in which the French invasion forces in Boulogne held Britain. Napoleon had massed troops on the coast facing Britain (from Brest to Ostend) but particularly at a camp on the coast in Boulogne. He had invested hugely in the building of a flotilla, on which to ferry his 'armée d'angleterre', so as to 'bring peace to London'. This latter encampment had been in place for nearly two years, and it kept a part of the British navy fixed to a station blockading the French coast. It also maintained the British public and its politicians in constant fear of invasion.

On his return to premiership in May 1804, William Pitt the Younger constructed a foreign policy designed to open a continental front, so as to render this camp untenable. Two weapons were used by Britain in this (initially diplomatic) offensive. One was to form aggressive coalitions against France (to which I shall return), and the second was to curry discord with France amongst the other countries of Europe.

In the latter respect she did not have to work too hard. France was inimical to Prussia because of her occupation of the left bank of the Rhine, as we have noted. Russia felt excluded from European affairs and was negative towards France both because of the Franco-Turkish rapprochement of 1802 (which Russia, because of her interest in the Near East, considered an act of war) and the execution of the Duc d'Enghien by Napoleon in the summer of 1804 (which led Russia to break off diplomatic relations and to expel the French ambassador, Hédouville).

As for Austria, she had been driven to the negotiating table twice when she was defeated by the French in both the First and Second Italian campaigns (1796 and 1800). Worse still, in 1804, Francis II, Holy Roman Emperor, had been obliged by Napoleon to abandon his Roman Empire and make do with merely an Austrian one, of which he was Francis I. That being said, Britain was not short of enemies either: Prussia had designs on George's III family seat, Hanover, and Russia found Britain's insolent behaviour on the high seas difficult to stomach. In short, there were many reasons for conflict.

Let us return to June 1805 – of all the countries in Europe, Austria was the one primarily affected (and dismayed) by Napoleon's actions in the Italian peninsula. In the first part of 1805, Austria had remained circumspect, trying where possible to live with French influence in northern Italy. Indeed, a first reaction to the news that the Milan coronation could take place had been to accept it but to try to bargain (unsuccessfully) other concessions in Italy. It is true that there was a vocal lobby in Austria advocating war with France, notably Francis's wife, Maria Theresa, daughter of Ferdinand I of the Two Sicilies, the niece of Marie Antoinette and passionately francophobe, and also bellicose generals such as Mack and Zach.[2] They urged revenge for the affront in Italy, but they were for the moment held in check by voices of prudence. Archduke Charles, commander-in-chief of the Austrian army in Italy, urged caution and warned that Austria would not be ready to fight before (at the earliest) 1806. The Austrian army was in fact in a period of disorganisation and attempts at military reform had not been well received.

Russia, on the other hand, reacted aggressively to the annexation of Liguria: '[Napoleon] is insatiable,' Alexander is said to have exclaimed, 'his ambition knows no bounds; he is a scourge of the world; he wants war; well, he shall have it, and the sooner the better.'[3] In the first part of 1805, Britain had been hoping to bring Russia into a coalition against France. Agreements to that effect had already been signed on 11 April 1805, whereby both countries would raise a coalition army of 400,000 men and start a war against France to make her return to her borders of 1789.

All that was required for completion of the treaty was Russian Emperor Alexander's ratification. Alexander, however, was, on the one hand distrustful (and disdainful) of Britain's reasons for wanting an anti-French coalition, and on the other he had decided to establish Russia on the European stage by playing the role of arbiter in European disagreements (in which he was warmly encouraged by Napoleon). Alexander felt that he had a certain influence with the French emperor and could act as a go-between with Britain and France, thereby avoiding the coming conflict and bringing prestige to Russia for having brokered the peace. In fact, Alexander had never intended either to ratify the April talks with Britain or to fight. Indeed, instead of sending the Russian envoy, Novosiltsov, to London, he was in fact dispatching that diplomat to Paris to try to arrange a peace with Napoleon.

On hearing of the Ligurian annexation, however, Alexander angrily called off Novosiltsov's mission to Paris, and immediately returned to the treaty with Britain – the ratifications of the treaty were exchanged on 29 July. Napoleon was probably correct in his opinion that the taking of Liguria (and the key ports of Genoa and La Spezia) affected primarily Britain,[4] but Alexander felt that his prestige had been damaged. Whilst some historians (and indeed Napoleon himself), have maintained that the coalition was cemented by British gold, it is clear that, as Paul Schroeder and others have put it, even though the British and Russians planned the Third Coalition, it was Napoleon who brought it into being.[5]

With Russia and Britain now finally allied, all eyes turned to Austria. Napoleon for his part was convinced that he could compel Austria to do what he wanted. Perceiving Austria's reaction to the recent affairs in Italy as limp, he gave aggressive and disdainful instructions regarding Austria to his Minister for Foreign Relations, Talleyrand, in July and August of 1805. For example, when the French emperor learned of Austrian military preparations in Bohemia and the Tyrol (even before becoming aware of what he himself termed 'The Third Coalition') he wrote to Talleyrand on 7 August instructing him to demand that Austria disarm and to threaten war if Austria did not remain neutral.[6] Nor was Napoleon entirely wrong in thinking that he could force Austria to back down – even while making military preparations, the Austrian court dithered in the face of Napoleon's threats, remembering all too well Rivoli and Marengo.

Britain also found Austria hesitant. Attempts to get Francis to sign a treaty of alliance met with temporising.[7] As the British diplomat Leveson Gower wrote to his colleague Harrowby (29 June 1805) the Austrians appeared to be 'like little children who put off minute by minute taking their physick though they know that the dose must be taken at last'.[8] In the last-ditch Austro-British talks on 7 July, however, Austrian Foreign Minister Ludwig Cobenzl argued to his ruler that war was inevitable and that the chances for finding allies were diminishing. So Austria took its medicine and signed secretly with Russia and Britain on 8 August. In the end, in the face of severe threat and provocation, Austria could not but want to remain an independent, 'great' nation.

This bringing aboard of the Austrians and the constitution of the Third Coalition was perhaps Britain's greatest victory of 1805. For with it came the abandonment of the Boulogne invasion camp and the consequent freedom this gave to the fleet. Napoleon was never again able to muster enough money and manpower to relaunch the invasion plan. Trafalgar was perhaps a portent of the later battle at Austerlitz.

But what of Napoleon during this time? He was hovering in Boulogne in August 1805, awaiting the arrival of French ships of the line to cover the launch of his invasion flotilla. He was of course well aware of the critical diplomatic (and soon to be military) situation developing: his numerous letters to Talleyrand in August 1805 regarding Austria give eloquent witness to this.[9] Indeed he was already mentally (if not actually) preparing to face the menace from the south-east. If Austria were to move against France while he was in Britain, he could be cut off from the continent.

Even though apparently still set on invading Britain and waiting for the imminent arrival of Villeneuve, he was also (in great secret) setting in motion plans for dealing with the potential Austrian threat. In a letter of 18 August, Napoleon informed Talleyrand that he had already given the order for *18e de ligne* and *1er Hussard* regiments (not from Boulogne, but from Paris and Versailles respectively) to join other regiments similarly detached to Strasbourg. The ostensible reason was manoeuvres, but in reality they were there to prepare for the impending conflict.[10] The front was already moving from the Channel to the Rhine.

Napoleon then set about creating his own coalition. France was already allied to Spain, the Netherlands, and the tiny principality recently given to his sister, Piombino. To complete the party, Bavaria was also courted and won; Bavaria was the German state permanently threatened by Austria, but which had been protected by the 1797 Treaty of Teschen and which traditionally turned to France for aid. He also brought on board the small German states of Baden, Württemberg and Hesse Darmstadt (their closeness to Strasbourg brought them traditionally into France's sphere of influence). Of particular interest here was the permission for his troops to cross, and to be stationed on, these territories. Though he could not secure an alliance with Prussia, he sent Duroc to Berlin in an attempt to keep the Prussians neutral until he had dealt with the Austro-Russian problem. The bait offered to Prussia was the British king's other domain, Hanover, which had been in French hands since 1804. This was to prove sufficient to keep Prussia out of the coming war.

As we have seen above, Napoleon was aware of the international crisis developing – it is clear that even while the plans to invade England were in their final stages, he had begun to plan the German campaign in his mind. Tradition has it that Napoleon made a sudden decision and dictated to his intendant Daru all the particulars of the Austerlitz campaign on 13 August. Though this date is far too early (the real date was probably 28 August) and Napoleon could not have predicted much at that time, the *dictée* nevertheless launched the '7 torrents' (the term was coined by Napoleon) which were to sweep into southern Germany.

On 23 August Napoleon had already written to Talleyrand, stating: 'I'm moving as fast as I can. I'm striking my camps . . . and on 23 September I shall have 200,000 men in Germany . . . I'm marching on Vienna.'[11] With one week to organise his troops and three to move them, Napoleon sent these '200,000 men across 600 kilometres, feeding, lodging and driving them to the Rhine. It was the first time in the history of warfare that such a mass of men moved so fast so efficiently and so far.'[12] The campaign was begun at a time of the year when generals were usually setting out their winter quarters. In the extraordinarily successful campaign around Ulm and the taking of Vienna, the victory was so swift, complete and startling that *The Times* in Britain brought out a special, first-ever Sunday edition (on 3 November) to bring the news of General Mack's capitulation at Ulm, with the loss of 25,000 men and sixty-five cannon, all without firing a shot.

After such catastrophic results, Francis would have given up and sued for peace had it not been for his persistent hope that Alexander and the Russian army could bring revenge. As the French émigré commander with the Allied army, Langeron, noted in his memoirs, 'it was a game of double or quits in which Francis hoped to win back some pride.'[13]

The Battle of Austerlitz and its Immediate Aftermath

That the battle of Austerlitz, which took place on 2 December 1805, exactly a year to the day after the religious coronation in Paris, was Napoleon's greatest victory can be seen from the bald statistics. According to the military historian, Robert Goetz, the Russian army lost 21,000 men (killed, wounded and taken prisoner). The Austrians had 5,922 men 'hors de combat'.[14] According to recent French research, Napoleon's losses amounted to 1,537 men, or, to put it bluntly, Russian and Austrian losses were eighteen times those of the French.[15]

The news of the victory at Austerlitz was sent via a telegraph from Strasbourg on 9 December. It reached Paris on the 10th and was published in the *Moniteur* newspaper on the 11th. 'The emperor has beaten the Russians near Olmütz,' it tersely read. The following day's *Moniteur* noted that the battle was called by the troops 'The Battle of the Three Emperors'. In the end, Napoleon renamed the battle 'Austerlitz' after the baroque 'beau chateau' in which he was lodging at the time, which had once belonged to the great Austrian statesman, Kaunitz.[16] It was here too, in the oval room, that the ceasefire was signed, on 6 December.

On 20 December, *The Times* published a description of an epic three-day struggle, during which the Allies were successful. The next day, a translation of Napoleon's famous Austerlitz proclamation was printed with a commentary casting doubt on what it considered outrageous claims. On the following days, reports of a French victory were resolutely discounted, and claims were made about how the bulletins were 'even beginning to be doubted in Paris'. It was not until 31 December that the paper grudgingly accepted that it had been a crushing French victory.

It is true that the defeat of the Third Coalition was not all bad for Britain. The conflict in southern Germany and Austria had removed the menace to Britain's coasts. The British Foreign Secretary, George Canning, was certainly not entirely dejected – he wrote to Pitt on 4 January 1806, noting that things had not deteriorated after the battle:

> If the very worst happens that is now threatened . . . if Austria does make a separate peace, and is abolished as a Power, and if Prussia lies down and licks Bonaparte's feet, and is forgiven and gets Hanover assigned to her for her submission – still, with Russia unpledged to peace and committed in war, we are better off than we were before the Coalition took place.[17]

However, in terms of international relations, Britain was very isolated, with Russia weakened and Austria disarmed. It is no surprise that on the death of Pitt, his government fell and Fox set about negotiating peace with France.

As for Napoleon, when he finally returned to Paris from Vienna on 27 January 1806, there were plays, balls, operas and 'Vive l'Empereur's on all sides. Capitaine

Coignet wrote in his memoirs that crowds came out to greet the returning soldiers. Tents were erected on the Champs-Elysées and food and fine wine were served.[18] That the battle was his second and final 'sacre', his military consecration, can be seen from the imperial decree pronounced on 20 February 1806, in the afterglow of Austerlitz, making the basilica of Saint-Denis the site for the imperial tombs. The Napoleon dynasty would henceforth lie in death alongside the kings of France.

The Memorials

In the year following the battle, to match the fervour of public opinion, several grand architectural and civil engineering projects were begun in Paris to mark the extraordinary success of the Austro-German campaign. Some are well known, others less so.[19] There was of course the large column erected in the Place Vendôme. The project for this was first seriously launched by Napoleon as First Consul in 1803, in honour of Charlemagne. However, in the wake of Austerlitz, Vivant Denon, director of the Louvre (then known as the Musée Napoléon) proposed a bronze commemoration column to the Grande Armée. It was to be made from the canons taken at the battle. And the projected statue of Charlemagne was replaced by a statue of Napoleon. Subsequent British attempts to rival this meant that Nelson's Column in Trafalgar Square was to be '43 feet higher than Bonaparte's Column in the Place Vendome at Paris'. Just as the Austerlitz column was made from the bronze of Austrian cannon taken at the battle, so the capital of Nelson's Column was made from 'French guns captured by the great Admiral'.[20]

Other Parisian monuments to the Grande Armée were planned – an Austerlitz column was to be built in Sèvres, decorated by the famous manufactory's best artists. The Arc de Triomphe de l'Etoile was, in fact, originally to be a celebration of the Battle of Austerlitz. So too was the Carrousel Arch, built in haste in front of the Tuileries Palace in honour of the Grande Armée and upon which were set the bronze horses taken from Saint Mark's, Venice.[21]

Of particular interest amongst the lesser-known celebrations of the battle is the Madeleine Church. On the symbolic date of 2 December 1806, Napoleon signed an imperial decree at the Posen Camp advertising a competition for 'the building of a temple to the glory of the French army on the site of the Madeleine'. The building programme included a pediment inscribed with the words 'L'Empereur Napoléon aux soldats de la Grande Armée'. And on the inside there were to be marble tablets on which were inscribed the names of all the men (arranged in order of army corps and regiment) who had fought at the battles of Ulm, Austerlitz and Jena. Those who had died on these battlefields were to have their names inscribed in solid gold tablets – there were also to be lists of all the soldiers who took part, by order of departments, these on tablets of silver. To complete this memorial there were to have been bas-reliefs showing the regiments of the Grande Armée, statues of the Maréchals and all their trophies, and the 'flags, standards and drums' taken from the enemy. The grandiose project was not to be completed before the fall of the First Empire, and all that remains of its original Napoleonic foundation is the fresco above the main altar bearing, *inter alia*, the Emperor in his coronation robes.

So much for the immediate aftermath of the battle. What happened after the fall of the regime in 1815? Naturally there was little interest during the Restoration, and the battle would not have been one of the regular topics of conversation in exile on Saint Helena, unlike the First Italian campaign, Waterloo, or Napoleon's civic achievements. On the other hand, Austerlitz does figure widely (and triumphantly) in the historical works of the nineteenth century as a whole, and not just during the explicitly 'Napoleonic' Second Empire. I found a crude benchmark of this using a CD-ROM containing the full texts of important French historians of the nineteenth century.[22] A search for the word 'Austerlitz' surprisingly revealed a fairly constant interest throughout the century, with no falling off during Royalist or Republican times.

In his four-volume work, *Histoire de Napoléon*, the Baron de Norvins, writing during the reign of Charles X, mentions the battle ninety-four times. Albert Sorel in his seven-volume work, *Europe et la Révolution française*, writing during the Third Republic (a regime by no means favourable towards the First Empire) cites the name eighty-two times, and Ernest Hamel in his *Histoire du Premier Empire* (similarly of the Third Republic) cited the word fifty-five times. Quite naturally the battle is mentioned a massive 217 times in Adolphe Thiers's twenty-volume history of the Consulate and Empire, published in the period 1845–69 (and so mostly during the Second Empire). We may conclude therefore that academic historical interest in the conflict remained high.

It is however much more difficult to take the pulse of the French nation as a whole. In the immediate aftermath of Waterloo, all those who professed an interest in Napoleon did so in secret. It was not until the 1830s that (in addition to the covert, passive interest amongst the history-reading public) there occurred certain high-profile, political or public events celebrating Napoleon. In the later part of his reign, Louis-Philippe flirted heavily with the Napoleonic legend, trying to enlist Bonapartists in the support of his beleaguered regime.

Three of his gestures were particularly 'Napoleonic'. The first was the creation of a Napoleonic gallery of paintings at the Palace of Versailles. In fact a suite of a dozen or so interconnecting rooms, this gallery was a painted monument to the grandeur of the Consulate and Empire. The second gesture was the replacement of the statue of Henri IV on top of the Vendôme column (which had been put there during the reign of Louis XVIII) with one of Napoleon. The third was, of course, the fundamentally Napoleonic moment of the return of Napoleon's body to France from Saint Helena, the famous 'retour des cendres', which the French government organised with its British counterpart in 1840.[23]

Although these gestures did not do much to shore up Louis-Philippe's reign, they were enormously popular, particularly the 'retour des cendres'. 'It was greater than a Roman triumph,' noted Balzac the day after the event. Indeed there was nothing funereal about the occasion, with an immense crowd lining the streets, delighted, despite the freezing weather on 15 December 1840. This in many ways laid the foundations for the return of a Napoleonic regime ten years later. The power of these gestures was not lost on Louis-Napoleon, son of Josephine's daughter and Napoleon's brother, who tried to profit from this renewed Napoleonic atmosphere by attempting two *coup d'états*.

For his first *coup d'état* in Strasbourg in October 1836, Louis-Napoleon explicitly appealed to the military and had a proclamation printed for distribution, in which he described himself as the bearer of 'the sword of Austerlitz'. Louis evidently felt that the battle would still win him hearts and minds – at least amongst the military. His second *coup d'état*, at Boulogne in 1840, was timed to coincide with the return of Napoleon's body. Here again the sword of Austerlitz was to play a part; on Saint Helena, Napoleon had instructed Bertrand, to hand the 'sword of Austerlitz' to his son, the King of Rome. Bertrand did not do so in 1821 on his return from Saint Helena. Since the King of Rome was now dead, Bertrand now presented the sword to Louis-Philippe so that it could be deposited with the emperor's body at Les Invalides. This outraged Bonapartists, especially Louis-Napoleon – the sword should never be in the hands of a dynasty that had replaced Napoleon. He wrote to *The Times* in May 1840 saying that 'The sword of Austerlitz should never be in enemy hands; it must remain where it can be brandished in the day of danger for the glory of France.'

As at Strasbourg, a pre-printed proclamation vaunted: 'I shall not halt until I have recovered the sword of Austerlitz'. To celebrate the return of the emperor's body, an illustrated handbill was published in 1841, explicitly linking the column and the 'retour des cendres'.[24] And in 1840, the recently founded railway company, the Compagnie d'Orléans, built and named its flagship Paris railway station after the battle (incidentally, Waterloo station in London was not built until 1848). Clearly Austerlitz was in the air, and clearly those who wielded the name thought that they did so to great effect.

When, eleven years later, Napoleon III established his imperial regime with a bloody coup, he did so on 2 December. The reference was twofold – his uncle's religious coronation but also the latter's military consecration. However, Louis was no Napoleon. We know that he was deeply shocked (and later scarred) by the violence which had accompanied his coup, his own 'Austerlitz' commemoration, when 27,000 people were arrested and sentenced. There were many deaths on the barricades in Paris and in the provinces – when his explicitly Napoleonic, Second Empire was established (and the bloody December coup out of the way), Napoleon III no longer had use for violence or military metaphors. He wanted his regime to be characterised by the catchphrase 'L'Empire, c'est la paix'.

In the salons the paintings were of love and beauty. Gone were the scenes of Napoleon's military campaigns. Indeed, Napoleon III's bourgeois, respectable regime, characterised by its warm relations with Britain, found itself particularly embarrassed by the aggressive elements of Napoleon I's history. Adolph Thiers, in many ways the quintessentially Second Empire historian, saw clearly the dilemma with respect to battles such as Austerlitz. That battle was not (on the surface) a battle of defence, unlike the great patriotic victories of 1792 when the *patrie* had been in danger. Thiers sensed this tension and felt obliged to argue the point, noting (perhaps not entirely convincingly) that there was no difference between a battle of aggression and a battle of defence, claiming that whilst it was virtuous to defend one's country when it was endangered, it was just as good to devote yourself to making it great and glorious.

However, for Napoleon III, there were to be no more wars for greatness and glory. There exists an emblematic engraving showing Napoleon III receiving politicians from the French provinces and gesturing through the window to the Vendôme column. Although the column is clearly important, the link made is familial and the context is political, not military. The Empire remains Napoleonic, mindful of its veterans, but it is peaceful, above all. The column continued to play a role as the focus of huge celebrations; one such was the visit of Queen Victoria and Prince Albert to France in 1854. It was, of course, the site for celebration for the victories over Austria at Magenta and Solferino. It is not, however, Austerlitz that is being celebrated, but rather the army. If Austerlitz is perceived at all, it is almost as a watermark.

Indeed, the name of the Vendôme column itself provides us with a 'weather vane' for the (waning) interest in Austerlitz. Over the nineteenth century, it changed from 'Colonne d'Austerlitz' to 'Victory Column', and then finally 'Colonne de la Grande Armée'. The latter (less Napoleonic) name came about because the monument came to be used by veterans as a place of commemoration on the anniversary of Napoleon's death, 5 May, and for Saint Napoleon, 15 August. The battle of Austerlitz became subsumed by the figure of the Grande Armée. When Balzac came to write about the column, he described it thus: 'The city of Paris has a great mast, made entirely of bronze, with sculpted Victories and Napoleon as its lookout.' Austerlitz is nowhere to be seen.[25] The column now became known as the Vendôme Column, after the square in which it is placed. Austerlitz had begun to slip in obscurity.

This process has continued; there was naturally a certain amount of interest during the first centenary of the battle in 1905. D'Alombert and Colin's fundamental seven-volume work on the battle dates from this period.[26] However, a glance at Caldwell's two-volume bibliography of works on Napoleon shows that very little has been written on the battle since:[27] books on Austerlitz occupy a single page (as do those on Marengo) whereas Waterloo has five pages. Even bearing in mind the huge Anglophone interest in the latter battle, there is less French interest in Austerlitz than in Waterloo. Perhaps the reason for the massive weighting in favour of Waterloo is what has been called the 'culture of defeat' surrounding the Belgian battle.[28] Waterloo also has the unique position in French collective memory as the defeat to be avenged, and is used for political purposes at various times.

For Austerlitz these days, there is merely the station and the bridge. Even the annual re-enactment at France's prestigious military academy, Saint-Cyr, every 2 December, is little known outside military circles. Indeed, in these Republican times, commemorations of this sort in France, particularly Napoleonic ones, are no longer considered tasteful – despite the popularity of military re-enactments elsewhere in Europe. The bicentenary of Austerlitz was commemorated in the Czech Republic with great pomp – there seemed to be no difficulty in celebrating a great Austro-Russian 'defeat'. In France, there have been no national acts of remembrance, either for Austerlitz (a battle whose name appears on more than one French regimental standard) or for any other of the Napoleonic bicentenaries to date.

It is perhaps worthwhile wondering at the cause of such reticence in France with respect to the Napoleonic bicentenaries. First of all, perhaps Napoleonic bicentenaries do not provide enough political 'capital'; perhaps French politicians are concerned about appearing triumphalist in these days of European partnership. It is possibly felt in French political circles that Napoleon is too hot to handle, a 'dictator's dictator' – a criticism that dates back to Napoleonic times themselves. Whilst it is true that Napoleon was not seen in such a positive light in certain countries – Spain, Prussia, even Italy – these feelings largely belong to the past. As the Czech event shows, it is possible to commemorate Napoleonic history in a European context without triumphalism.

In Britain, 2005 seemed like one long commemoration of Nelson and Trafalgar, and there were events at which both Spain and France were present. Viewed from the 'other side' of the channel, these events have not been perceived as triumphalist. It therefore appears perfectly possible to 'remember' without 'enthusiasm'. We at the Fondation Napoleon hold that Napoleon (like Nelson) is a key figure in our common history – not forgetting, however, that there are certain national sensitivities. He is no longer an object of polemic but an object of history, one to be studied with rigour and openness of spirit. The most important point (and this is one which is not understood by the French government) is that a commemoration – which is not a celebration – cannot be undertaken in any context other than European. If war is the continuation of politics by other means, then commemoration is the continuation of history by other means. As such, it is one of the best ways of juxtaposing, and trying to understand, the different political conceptions of Europe and European society today.[29]

Notes

❦

Introduction

1 For a good selection of essays exploring the new scholarship, see D Cannadine (ed), *Trafalgar in History: A Battle and Its Afterlife* (London, 2006); D Cannadine, (ed), *Admiral Lord Nelson: Context and Legacy* (London, 2005);*The Mariner's Mirror: Bicentenary of Trafalgar* (2005), No 2, p 91; *Trafalgar Chronicle: Year Book of the 1805 Club*, (2006) p 16. New biographies, such as Roger Knight, *Nelson: Pursuit of Victory*, (London, 2005); Andrew Lambert, *Nelson: Britannia's God of War* (London, 2004); Colin White, *Nelson: The Admiral*, (London, 2005); Terry Colman, *Nelson: The Man and the Legend* (London, 2001); E Vincent, *Nelson: Love and Fame* (New Haven, 2003); John Sugden, *Nelson: Quest for Glory* (London, 2004), Vol 1, are just a few of the books that appeared between 2001 and 2005.

Chapter 1

1 TS Jackson (ed), *Logs of the Great Sea Fights, 1794–1805*, 2 vols (London, 1899–1900), Vol 2, pp 139–327. Except where otherwise stated, all references to British logs are taken from this document.

2 W James, *The Naval History of Great Britain during the French Revolutionary and Napoleonic Wars*, 6 vols (London, 1837), Vol 3, pp 381–474. Although containing matters of detail unavailable elsewhere, the overall description suffers from the misidentification of several ships of the Combined Fleet. Many later publications repeated James's version of events.

3 AH Taylor, 'The Battle of Trafalgar', *The Mariner's Mirror*, Vol 36, No 4 (1950), pp 281–321. Captain (later Rear Admiral) Taylor undertook the research for the positions of the ships in Wyllie's Trafalgar Panorama. Originally intended for publication in book form, the 1950 *Mariner's Mirror* article described the whole of the battle and replaced James as the standard account, being widely used by later authors.

4 Log of T Atkinson, Master HMS *Victory*: Jackson, *Logs of the Great Sea Fights*, Vol 2, p 184.

5 C White, 'Nelson's 1805 Battleplan', *Journal of Maritime Research* (April 2002), <www.jmr.nmm.ac.uk>.

6 C Bridge (chairman), *Report of a Committee Appointed by the Admiralty to Examine and Consider the Evidence Relating to the Tactics Employed by Nelson at Trafalgar*. Cd 7120, (1913) (hereafter The Bridge Report). By the time of the centenary of Trafalgar in 1905, almost thirty plans had already been published of the positions of the opposing fleets. One of the main outcomes of the report was to provide a diagram of the commencement of the action at 12.00, to alter the model then on display at Greenwich and the plan shown on board HMS *Victory*.

Long neglected, this important analysis has at last begun to receive wider recognition.

7   D Wheeler, 'The Weather at the Battle of Trafalgar', *Weather*, Vol 40 (1985), pp 338–46.

8   R Monaque, *Latouche-Treville, L'Amiral qui defiait Nelson*, (Paris, 2000), p 573.

9   E Desbrière , *The Naval Campaign of 1805, Trafalgar*, trans and ed by C Eastwick, 2 vols (Oxford, 1933); essential for the Franco-Spanish accounts. Except where otherwise stated, all references to the logs and journals of the Combined Fleet are taken from this document.

10 E Fraser, *The Enemy at Trafalgar* (London, 1906).

11 *Defiance*: Letter from Midshipman C Reid, HMS *Defiance*, *The Mariner's Mirror*, Vol 9, No 1 (1923), p 60. *Defiance*: Letter from Midshipman C Campbell, HMS *Defiance*, *The Mariner's Mirror*, Vol 9, No 2 (1923), pp 119–20. *Thunderer*: Journal of Commander T Colby, HMS *Thunderer*, *The Mariner's Mirror*, Vol 13, No 3 (1927), pp 264–7.

12 *The Naval Chronicle*, Vol 21 (1809), p 23.

13 JS Corbett (ed), *Fighting Instructions, 1530–1816 Publications of the Navy Records Society*, Vol 29 (London, 1905) and JS Corbett (ed), *Signals and Instructions, 1776–1794* (London, 1909). Anson appears to have influenced the development of this formation, more commonly referred to in 1747 as a 'bow and quarter line', although Hawke was the first to establish it as a squadron formation whilst in the Mediterranean. The line of bearing was developed further in English tactical writings issued by Lord Howe in July 1778. One advantage of the tactic was to lessen concentration of fire against any single ship, dividing the impact of shot over the formation and reducing the chance of any ship sustaining significant damage before reaching close quarters with an enemy.

14 J Bourchier (ed), *Memoir of the Late Admiral Sir Edward Codrington*, 2 vols (London, 1873), p 77.

15 E Hughes (ed), *The Private Correspondence of Admiral Lord Collingwood*, (London, 1957), p 167.

16 WS Lovell, *Personal Narrative of Events from 1699 to 1815*, 2nd edn, (1879). Midshipman Badcock took the surname Lovell in 1840.

17 Vicomte de Morogue, *Tactique Navale ou Traite des Evolutions et des Signaux* (1763).

18 B Tunstall, *Naval Warfare in the Age of Sail: The Evolution of Fighting Tactics 1650–1850*, ed N Tracy (London, 1990), p 251.

19 Desbrière, *The Naval Campaign of 1805, Trafalgar*, p 167.

20 Ibid., p 400.

21 AH Taylor, 'Notes', *The Mariner's Mirror*, Vol 37, No 4, (1951), p 325.

22 The devastating power of the projectile that hit Nelson is often underestimated today. Contemporary tests showed that inside a 100-yard range the three-quarter-ounce ball could penetrate nearly five inches of solid oak.

23 Bourchier, *Memoir of the Late Admiral Sir Edward Codrington*, pp 60–8.

24 J Allen, *Memoir of the Life and Services of Admiral Sir William Hargood* (1841), pp 137–45.

25 Ibid., appendix E, 'Account of Lt Nicholas Harris of the Belleisle', pp 278–89.

26 Letter from Midshipman C Reid, HMS *Defiance, The Mariner's Mirror,* Vol 9, No 1 (1923), p 60.
27 Ibid., pp 119–20.

Chapter 2

1 See Cannadine, *Trafalgar in History.*
2 Anon to Melville, undated: National Archive of Scotland GD/51/2/372–3.
3 Tim Clayton and Phil Craig, *Trafalgar, the Men, the Battle, the Storm,* (London, 2004), p 43.
4 See Colin White (ed), *The Trafalgar Captains – Their Lives and Memorials* (Chatham, 2005).
5 They were: Hardy, Berry, Fremantle and Hope, who had served with Nelson in the Mediterranean in 1797–8 and subsequently; Tyler, who had been in the Baltic fleet in 1801 when Nelson was in command; Bayntun, Rutherford, Conn, Pellew and Hargood, who had served with him in the Mediterranean campaign of 1803–4; and Laforey, who had served with him on the chase to the West Indies earlier in 1805. Two of the frigate captains – Blackwood and Capel – had also served with him before.
6 Michael Duffy, '"All was Hushed Up": the Hidden Trafalgar', *The Mariner's Mirror,* Vol 91, No 2 (May 2005), pp 216–40, specifically p 234.
7 Michael Duffy, 'The Gunnery at Trafalgar: Training, Tactics or Temperament?', *Journal of Maritime Research* (July 2005), <www.jmr.nmm.ac.uk>.
8 For a full analysis of the performance of each ship at Trafalgar, see Duffy, '"All was Hushed Up"'.
9 See White, *Nelson: The Admiral,* especially pp 88–9.
10 Sir Nicholas Harris Nicolas, *The Dispatches and Letters of Lord Nelson* (London, 1844–7), Vol 7, p 71.
11 Codrington: Bourchier, *Memoir of Sir Edward Codrington* (London, 1873), p 52.
12 For an examination of these books, and an analysis of their contents see C White (ed), *Nelson: The New Letters* (Woodbridge, 2005).
13 All these orders, with the exception of the last, are printed by Nicolas, *The Dispatches and Letters,* Vol 7, pp 101–7. The orders about night sailing are in the Clive Richards Collection: CRC/66.
14 Fremantle's Journal, *The Mariner's Mirror,* Vol 16, (1930).
15 Nelson's Public Order Book: RNM (Admiralty Library) MS200.
16 For examples of these notes, see White, *Nelson: The New Letters,* especially pp 53–66 and 326–9.
17 Nelson to Collingwood, 7 October 1805, Nicolas, *The Dispatches and Letters,* Vol 7, p 83.
18 See White, *Nelson: The New Letters,* pp 368–80 and Roger Knight, *The Pursuit of Victory, The Life and Times of Horatio Nelson,* (London, 2005).
19 The British wrongly thought that the Combined Fleet was commanded by Napoleon's Minister for Marine, Denis Decrès.
20 Bayntun to Nelson, 25 September 1805, British Library: Add Mss 34931.

21 From a copy in Keats's own handwriting in the Somerset Record Office: DD/CPL/41. Printed, with some textual alterations, in Nicolas, *The Dispatches and Letters*, Vol 7, p 241.

22 White, *Nelson: The Admiral*, p 160; White, 'Nelson's 1805 Battleplan'. The plan is in the collection of the National Maritime Museum, BRP/6.

23 Nelson to Emma Hamilton, 30 September 1805, Nicolas, *The Dispatches and Letters*, Vol 7, p 60.

24 In 1913, for example, the Admiralty appointed a special committee to examine the memorandum and to establish to what extent Nelson succeeded in carrying out his plan on 21 October.

25 White, *Nelson: The Admiral*. The text of all the main battleplans is printed as an appendix, pp 194–210.

26 Julian Corbett, *The Campaign of Trafalgar* (London, 1910).

27 For full text, see: Nicolas, *The Dispatches and Letters*, Vol 7, pp 89–92; White, *Nelson: The Admiral*, pp 208–9.

28 The 1805 'West Indies' plan has not survived. For a reconstruction, from other evidence, of what it might have contained, see White, *Nelson: The Admiral*, p 148.

29 Quoted in a letter from Blackwood to his wife: Nicolas, *The Dispatches and Letters*, Vol 7, pp 226–7.

30 George Hewson to his father, 2 November 1805. Houghton Library, Harvard. ENG 196.5 f.134.

31 Message to Fremantle: Minutes of Lt Green of HMS *Neptune*, Huntington Library, California: STG Box 150 (1). Message to the captains: Nicolas, *The Dispatches and Letters*, Vol 7, p 150.

32 Signal: Tunstall, *Naval Warfare in the Age of Sail*, p 251. Codrington: Nicolas, *The Dispatches and Letters*, Vol 7, p 154. Dumanoir: *The Times*, 2 January 1806. Spanish Plan: Houghton ENG 196.5 f.161.

33 Hewson: see note 30 above. Collingwood: Nicolas, *The Dispatches and Letters*, Vol 7, p 241.

34 JH and Edith Hubback, *Jane Austen's Sailor Brothers* (London, 1906), p 156.

Chapter 3

1 J González-Aller Hierro, 'La campaña de Trafalgar (1804–1805)', *Corpus documental conservado en los archivos españoles*, 2 vols (Madrid, 2005), Vol 2, p 1,018.

2 The sources on the battle and its European context have been thoroughly reviewed in a magnificent documentary catalogue by Admiral José Ignacio González-Aller Hierro.

3 The bibliography on the situation of the three navies in 1805 is too wide, but see Cannadine, *Trafalgar in History*, also J Blanco Nuñez, P Castro Martin and E Garcia Hernán (eds), *Actas XXI Congreso Internacional de Historia Militar: 'Poder terrestre y poder naval en la época de la batalla de Trafalgar'* (Madrid, 2006); A Guimerá, A Ramos and G Butrón (eds), *Trafalgar y el mundo atlántico* (Madrid, 2004); A Guimerá Ravina and V Peralta Ruiz (eds), *El equilibrio de los imperios: de Utrecht a Trafalgar* (Madrid, 2005). All these studies have a selected bibliography.

4   A Guimerá Ravina, 'Trafalgar y la marinería española', in Guimerá Ravina and Peralta Ruiz, *El equilibrio de los imperios*, pp 819–38.

5   A Escaño, *Ideas del Excmo Sr D Antonio de Escaño sobre un plan de reforma para la marina militar de Spain. Publícalas . . . su ayudante. . . teniente de navío de the Armada Nacional*, (Cádiz, 1820).

6   Escaño to Godoy, 5 November 1805; in González-Aller Hierro, 'La campaña de Trafalgar', p 1,077.

7   JM Carla, *Navíos en secuestro. La escuadra española del océano en Brest, 1799–1802* (Madrid, 1951); C Fernández Duro, *La Armada española desde la unión de los reinos de Castilla y Aragón*, facsimile edn (Madrid, 1973), Vol 8, pp 305–65; and Guimerá Ravina, 'Trafalgar y la marinería española'.

8   See the proceedings of the International Conference Bloqueos navales y operations anfibias en las guerras de la Revolución y el Imperio, Ferrol, 3–7 July 2007, ed A Guimerá and JM Blanco (forthcoming).

9   Kerautret: JM Humber and B Ponsonnet (eds), *Napoléon et la Mer. Un Rêve d'Empire* (Paris, 2004) p 181.

10 See A Rodríguez, 'Las innovaciones artilleras y tácticas españolas en la campaña de Trafalgar', in Blanco, Núñez-Castro and Martin-Garcia Hernan *Actas XXI Congreso Internacional de Historia Militar*, pp 539–52.

11 FP Pavía, *Galería biográfica de los generales de marina, jefes y personajes notables que figuraron en la misma corporación desde 1700 a 1868* (Madrid, 1873), Vol 2, p 134.

12 FP Cuadrado y de Roo, *Elogio histórico del Excelentísimo Señor Don Antonio de Escaño, Teniente General de Marina . . . por Don . . . ministro plenipotenciario, etc., etc.* (Madrid, 1852); J Vargas y Ponce, *Elogio histórico de D Antonio de Escaño*, ed JF Guillén (Madrid, 1962); and González-Aller Hierro, 'La campaña de Trafalgar', pp 925, 933 and 939.

13 González-Aller Hierro, 'La campaña de Trafalgar', pp 925, 933 and 939.

14 P Masson, *Histoire de la Marine. Tome I. L'Ère de la Voile* (Paris, 1992), 2nd edn, pp 360–61.

15 A Guimerá, 'Gravina y el liderazgo naval de su tiempo', in Guimerá, Ramos and Butrón, *Trafalgar y el mundo atlántico*, pp 233–56.

16 Ibid.

17 See AR Rodríguez González, 'Algunos apuntes sobre el combate de Trafalgar', and V San Juan, 'La controvertida virada por redondo en Trafalgar', both in *Revista General de Marina*, No 249 (2005), pp 299–310 and 311–28.

18 González-Aller Hierro, 'La campaña de Trafalgar'.

19 Lieutenant-General Mazarredo defended a similar period of training, when he took command of the Mediterranean Fleet; Mazarredo to Antonio Valdés, 27 August 1795, in Guimerá Ravina, 'Trafalgar y la marinería española'.

20 Escaño to Godoy, 17 December 1805, in González-Aller Hierro, 'La campaña de Trafalgar', p 1,191.

21 Ibid.

22 See also M-A Gundul Hervás, 'Estudio sobre las evoluciones de los navíos *Argonauta* y *Príncipe de Asturias* en el combate naval de Trafalgar', in *Revista General de Marina*, No 249 (2005), pp 317–28.

23 Collingwood to W Marsden, 21 October 1805, in González-Aller Hierro, 'La campaña de Trafalgar', p 977.

24 Collingwood to W Marsden, 24 October 1805; in 28 October 1805, in González-Aller Hierro, 'La campaña de Trafalgar', pp 999 and 1,031; other news on pp 1,383 and 1,516.

25 Escaño to E MacDonnell, 8 September 1806, and Escaño to Godoy, 22 November 1805, in González-Aller Hierro, 'La campaña de Trafalgar', pp 1,077ff.

26 A Guimerá Ravina, 'Imitando al enemigo: el plan de reforma naval de Antonio de Escaño (1807)', in *Homenaje a Dolores Higueras* (Madrid, forthcoming).

27 See Trafalgar dossier in *La aventura de la Historia*, No 48 (October 2005).

Chapter 4

1 See Duffy, '"All was Hushed Up"'.

2 'Souvenirs d'un Marin de la République', Part 2, *Revue des Deux Mondes*, Vol 28 (1905), p 418; Jackson, *Logs of the Great Sea Fights* (London, 1900) , Vol 2, p 214; Nicolas, *The Dispatches and Letters*, Vol 7, p 288.

3 Jackson, *Logs of the Great Sea Fights*, Vol 2, p 322.

4 National Maritime Museum, MS 80/201, Log entry of Richard Anderson.

5 A Schom, *Trafalgar. Countdown to Battle 1803–1805* (London, 1990), p 198; G Desdevises du Dezert, *La Marine Espagnol pendant la campagne de Trafalgar* (Toulouse, 1898), pp 6–7; Desbrière, *The Naval Campaign of Trafalgar*, Vol 2, p 105; JI González-Aller Hierro, 'Some Strategies and Tactics Regarding the Trafalgar Campaign', *Journal for Maritime Research* (26 April 2005), n 18, <http://www.jmr.nmm.ac.uk>.

6 González-Aller Hierro 'Some Strategies and Tactics Regarding the Trafalgar Campaign', n 13; Desbrière, *The Naval Campaign of Trafalgar*, Vol 2, p 109.

7 Desbrière, *The Naval Campaign of Trafalgar*, Vol 2, pp 142–3.

8 J de Zulueta, 'Trafalgar – The Spanish View', *The Mariner's Mirror*, Vol 66 (1980), pp 300–1.

9 E Fraser, *Sailors whom Nelson Led* (London, 1913), p 258.

10 Nicolas, *The Dispatches and Letters*, Vol 7, p 80.

11 Nicolas, *The Dispatches and Letters*, Vol 7, p 139.

12 The author has explored this issue in more depth in his articles '"All was Hushed Up"', and 'The Hidden Trafalgar – Dull Winds or Dull Captains?', *The Mariner's Mirror*, Vol 92 (2006), pp 226–30.

13 Royal Naval Museum, Portsmouth, 1963/1, Benjamin Stevenson, *Victory*, 5 November 1805. See also Duffy, 'The Gunnery at Trafalgar'.

14 'Souvenirs d'un Marin de la République', p 419.

15 Jackson, *Logs of the Great Sea Fights*, Vol 2, p 241.

16 Desbrière, *The Naval Campaign of Trafalgar*, Vol 2, pp 145–6.

17 H Robinson, *Sea Drift* (Portsea, 1858), p 216.

18 'The Battle of Trafalgar', *English Historical Review*, Vol 5 (1890), pp 768–9.

19 C Ekins, *Naval Battles from 1744 to the Peace in 1814* (London, 1824), p 277.

20 Nicolas, *The Dispatches and Letters*, Vol 7, p 95.

21 Desbrière, *The Naval Campaign of Trafalgar*, Vol 2, p 73.

22 J Ehrman, *The Younger Pitt* (London, 1996) , Vol 3, p 808.

23 JK Laughton, *Letters and Papers of Charles, Lord Barham* (London, 1911) , Vol 3, p 342.
24 MA Lewis (ed), *A Narrative Of My Professional Adventures by Sir William Henry Dillon* (Navy Records Society, 1956), Vol 2, p 52.
25 GL Newnham Collingwood, *A Selection from the Public and Private Correspondence of Vice Admiral Lord Collingwood* (London, 1837), Vol 1, p 226.
26 Escaño, *Ideas del Excmo*, p 11. I am grateful to Agustín Guimera for bringing this document to my attention.
27 Details from Pam and Derek Ayshford, *The Ayshford Complete Trafalgar Roll*, CD-ROM (Brussels, 2004); Patrick Marioné, *The Complete Navy List of the Napoleonic Wars 1793–1815*, CD-ROM (Brussels, 2003).
28 *The Times*, 22 October 1846, p 8.

Chapter 5

1 I would like to take this opportunity to express my gratitude to Michael Duffy, Nicolas Rodger and Colin White on the one hand, and to José Ignacio Gonzalez-Aller Hierro and Agustín Guimera on the other.
2 Napoleon, *Correspondance publiée par ordre de l'Empereur Napoléon III* (Paris, 1858), No 9179, 4 September 1805.
3 Napoleon, *Correspondence*, No 9220.
4 The *Principe de Asturias* and the *Santa Ana* may be magnificent vessels, but the *Santissima Trinidad* and the *Rayo*, on the other hand have grave shortcomings.
5 Nelson's death is often attributed to Sergeant Robert Guillemard of the 16th Regiment of Infantry. This is a longstanding hoax, the hero in question never lived except in the imagination of the Toulon-born writer, Alexandre Lardier, author of this fictitious character's *Memoirs*. See R Rose 'Who Shot Nelson, Who Shot Robert Guillemard?', *The Mariner's Mirror*, Vol 90 (2004), pp 236–7.

Chapter 6

1 For a brief, up-to-date survey with a full bibliography see Clive Emsley, *Britain and the French Revolution* (London, 2000).
2 The best survey of the militia is JR Western, *The English Militia in the Eighteenth Century: The Story of a Political Issue 1660–1802* (London, 1965).
3 *Leeds Intelligencer*, 30 May 1803. It had been possible for British people to travel on continental Europe during the wars of the eighteenth century. The French Revolution, with its ideological element, seriously hampered such travel. Napoleon followed this by ordering the internment of all Britons in France on 23 May 1803. See Michael Lewis, *Napoleon and his British Captives* (London, 1962).
4 *The Times*, 11 January 1805. The comment was made with reference to the Middlesex election during which, according to *The Times*, 'pair-makers' were said to be voting for the radical Sir Francis Burdett, and recruiting sergeants and police officers were touring the pubs seeking them out. One Bow Street constable allegedly picked up nineteen deserters from one regiment in two days.

5   JW Fortescue, *The County Lieutenancies and the Army, 1803–1814* (London, 1909), Appendix I, p 292; Captain BH Liddell Hart (ed), *The Letters of Private Wheeler, 1809–1828* (London, 1951). Edward Costello also enlisted from Militia, see Antony Brett-James (ed), *Edward Costello: Adventures of a Soldier: Written by Himself* (London, 1967).

6   Fortescue, *County Lieutenancies*, Appendix I, p 292; Christopher Hibbert (ed), *The Recollections of Rifleman Harris*, (London, 1970).

7   Godfrey Davies, *Wellington and his Army* (Oxford, 1954) pp 69–71.

8   Ann Kussmaul (ed), *The Autobiography of Joseph Mayett of Quainton 1783–1839*, Buckinghamshire Record Society, No 23 (Buckinghamshire, 1986), p 24.

9   The best survey of the volunteers is Austin Gee, *The British Volunteer Movement, 1794–1814* (Oxford, 2003).

10 Linda Colley, *Britons: Forging the Nation 1707–1837* (New Haven, 1992); JE Cookson, *The British Armed Nation, 1793–1815* (Oxford, 1997). The latter stresses the impact on the different 'nations' – English, Welsh, Scots and Irish – within 'Britain'.

11 Freeling to Sullivan, 7 March 1804, National Archives, HO 42.67.

12 The force, under the command of Lord Cawdor, which marched against Tate, was reported to consist of 100 Cardigan Militia, 100 Pembrokeshire Fencibles, 190 Knox's Fencibles, 150 sailors and fifty Castlemartin Yeomanry Cavalry, giving a total of 590. This was augmented by some 150 gentlemen and volunteers. EH Stuart-Jones, *The Last Invasion of Britain* (Cardiff, 1950), p 108; the legend of the Welsh women in their black hats and red capes, mistaken by the French for British troops, is discussed on pp 116–18. It seems possible that women were strategically placed overlooking the sands on which Tate surrendered to give the impression of a large British force. Fencibles were regular regiments recruited specifically for the duration of the war. The early years of the war against the French Revolution were the last time that such regiments were recruited.

13 *The Times*, 7 February 1804.

14 Lee to Winter, 24 August, Winter to Huskisson, 28 August and Huskisson to Smyth, 30 August 1805, National Archives, HO 42.81.

15 Clive Emsley, 'The Military and Popular Disorder in England 1790–1801', *Journal of the Society for Army Historical Research*, Vol 61 (1983), Part 1, pp 10–21, and Part 2, pp 96–112; see especially pp. 104–7.

16 Hawkesbury to Mayor of Chesterfield, 10 July 1805, National Archives, HO 43.15.228–9; Hawkesbury to Lieutenant Colonel Jebb, 18 July 1805, National Archives, HO 43.15.233–4.

17 Hawkins to?, 12 December 1804, National Archives, HO 42.83; Fletcher to King 16 January 1805 and 7 March 1805, HO 42.82, and 16 February 1805, HO 42.80.

18 Bennett to Yorke, 29 December 1803, National Archives, HO 42.74.30; see also King to Bennett (draft), 30 December 1803, HO 42.74.35; and Memo to the Earl of Stamford 'In Lord Stamford's of 5th. January 1804', HO 42.78.

19 Wright to Yorke, 15 February 1804, National Archives, HO 42.78.

20 Wright to Yorke, 4 February 1804, National Archives, HO 42.78; *The Times*, 28 November 1804, p 3.

21 Gee, *The British Volunteer Movement*, pp 166–7.

22 Hawkesbury to Lord Mountedgecombe, 19 October 1804, National Archives, HO 43.15.74–75; Hickens to Rashleigh, 31 October 1804, HO 42.83, forwarded to HO by Mountedgecombe.

23 HFB Wheeler and AM Broadley, *Napoleon and the Invasion of England: The Story of the Great Terror* (London, 1908).

24 For an account emphasising the danger of the revolutionary threat see Roger Wells, *Insurrection: The British Experience, 1795–1803* (Gloucester, 1983).

25 Notary's report, 18 January 1804, National Archives, HO 42.78. For Notary's career see J Ann Hone, *For the Cause of Truth: Radicalism in London, 1796–1821* (Oxford, 1982), pp 63–4, 111–15 and 137–8.

26 Marianne Elliott, 'The "Despard Conspiracy" Reconsidered', *Past and Present*, Vol 75 (1977), pp 46–61.

27 Old Bailey Sessions Papers, 14 September 1803 <http://www.Oldbaileyonline.org> (t.18030914-28).

28 Notary's report, 16, 18 and 23 February 1804, National Archives, HO 42.78.

29 For an excellent discussion of contrasting attitudes to Napoleon see Stuart Semmel, *Napoleon and the British* (New Haven and London, 2004).

30 Report of Major Reynolds, 7 April 1798, National Archives, WO 30.62.

31 Sheila Sutcliffe, *Martello Towers* (Newton Abbot, 1972); WH Clements, *Towers of Strength: The Story of the Martello Towers* (Barnsley, 1999).

32 PAL Vine, *The Royal Military Canal: An Historical Account of the Waterway and Military Road from Shoreditch in Kent to Cliff End in Sussex* (Newton Abbot, 1972).

33 Richard Glover, *Britain at Bay: Defence against Bonaparte, 1803–1814* (London, 1973) p 54.

34 Peter Bloomfield, *Kent and the Napoleonic Wars* (Gloucester, 1987), pp 48–50, and document 27.

35 Clive Emsley, *British Society and the French Wars, 1793–1815* (London, 1979) p 133. PK O'Brien, 'The Impact of the Revolutionary and Napoleonic Wars, 1793–1815, on the Long-Run Growth of the British Economy', *Review: Ferdinand Braudel Center*, Vol 12, No 3 (1989), pp 335–95; on p 336 O'Brien estimates that between 1801 and 1811 between 11 and 14 per cent of the male population aged between fifteen and forty years were recruited into the army and navy. Gee, *The British Volunteer Movement*, pp 68–9, concludes that roughly one-fifth of the adult male civilian population was enrolled in a volunteer corps in 1803.

36 Sir Charles Oman, *Wellington's Army*, (London, 1912), pp 375–83, lists 108 such, but admits that the list is incomplete.

37 See, for example, John Cartwright, *England's Aegis; or the Military Energies of the Constitution* (London, 1806). The fact that women could not serve as 'military defenders of their country', was one of the reasons he gave for denying the vote to women, see John Cartwright, *An Appeal, Civil and Military, on the Subject of the English Constitution* (London, 1799), p 17.

Chapter 7

1 Colley, *Britons. Forging the Nation*. To paraphrase the title of Paul Langford's *A Polite and Commercial People: England, 1727–1783* (Oxford, 1992).

2   J Morvan, *Le Soldat Impérial (1800–1814)*, 2 vols (Paris, 1904) Vol 1, p 290.
3   Howard G Brown, *Ending the French Revolution. Violence, Justice and Repression from the Terror to Napoleon* (Charlottesville and London, 2006), Part 3.
4   Morvan, *Soldat Impérial*, Vol 2, pp 10–11.
5   Ibid., Vol 1, p 288.
6   J Elting, *Swords Around a Throne: Napoleon's Grande Armée* (New York, 1988), p 56.
7   Morvan, *Soldat Impérial*, Vol 1, pp. 446–54.
8   Isser Woloch, 'Napoleonic Conscription: State Power and Civil Society', *Past and Present*, Vol 3 (1986). Alan Forrest, *Conscripts and Deserters: The French Army and Society during the Revolution and Empire* (Oxford, 1989).
9   Clive Emsley, *Gendarmes and the State in Nineteenth-Century Europe* (Oxford, 1999), Part 1.
10 Elting, *Swords Around a Throne*, pp 57–8.
11 Morvan, *Soldat Impérial*, Vol 1, pp 276–83.
12 Ibid., Vol 1, pp 287–89.
13 On the camp itself and its construction, see FE Beaucour, *Quand Napoléon Régnait à Pont-de-Briques* (Levalois, 1978).
14 Elting, *Swords Around a Throne*, pp 59–60.
15 Morvan, *Soldat Impérial*, Vol 1, pp 285–6.
16 Ibid., Vol 1, pp 291–3.
17 Ibid., Vol 1, p 298.
18 H Lachouque, *The Anatomy of Glory: Napoleon and his Guard*, English trans (London, 1962) p 27.
19 Lachouque, *Anatomy of Glory*, p 51.
20 Morvan, *Soldat Impérial*, Vol 2, pp 22–3.

Chapter 8

1   Since the battle itself was beyond the scope of this article, readers desiring information on the military events are invited to consult the following works: Jacques Garnier, *Austerlitz, 2 décembre 1805* (Paris, 2005); Robert Goetz, *1805: Austerlitz: Napoleon and the Destruction of the Third Coalition* (London, 2005); Ian Castle, *Austerlitz 1805: The Fate of Empires* (Oxford, 2002); and David Chandler, *Austerlitz 1805: Battle of the Three Emperors* (London, 1990).
2   See Napoleon, *Correspondance*, No 9,038, 3 August 1805.
3   Quoted in John Holland Rose, *The Life of Napoleon* (London, 1913), Vol 2, p 11.
4   Napoleon, *Correspondance*, No 8,889, 14 June 1805, to Champagny.
5   Paul Schroeder, *The Transformation of European Politics* (Oxford, 1994), p 264. See also John M Sherwig, *Guineas and Gunpowder: British Foreign Aid in the Wars with France* (Cambridge, MA, 1969), p 160.
6   Napoleon, *Correspondance*, No 9,055, 7 August 1805.
7   During the negotiations, Austria did indeed play for time, demanding that the independence of Piedmont be an integral part of negotiations with France.
8   Quoted in Ehrmann, *The Younger Pitt*, Vol 3, p 784.

9   Napoleon, *Correspondance*, No 9,038, 9,039, 9,041, 9,055, 9,062, 9,068, 9,070 etc.

10 Napoleon, letter to Talleyrand, 18 August 1805, Archives Nationales, Paris, 400 AP 139, published in PC Alombert and J Colin, *La Campagne de 1805 en Allemagne*, new edn, ed Jacques Garnier (Paris, 2002), Vol 1, p 66; Berthier Report, 15 August, cited in ibid., p 67.

11 Napoleon, *Correspondance*, No 9,117.

12 Pierre Charrier, *Le Maréchal Davout* (Paris, 2005), p 129.

13 Alexandre Andrault de Langeron, 'Journal Inédit de la Campagne de 1805', in Thierry Rouillard (ed), *Austerlitz. Relations de la Bataille d'Austerlitz* (Paris, 1998), p 156, n 3.

14 Goetz, *1805: Austerlitz*, p 278.

15 Danielle and Bernard Quintin, *2 décembre 1805. Austerlitz: Dictionnaire Biographique des Soldats de Napoléon Tombés au Champ d'Honneur* (Paris, 2005), p 258.

16 Napoleon, *Correspondance*, No 9,538, 3 December 1805, to Joseph his brother.

17 John Holland Rose, *Pitt and Napoleon: Essays and Letters* (London, 1912), p 333.

18 Jean Mistler (ed), *Les Cahiers du Capitaine Coignet* (Paris, 1968), p 120. Despite the torrential rain (which ruined the food), the soldiers had a fine time.

19 See Edouard Driault, *Napoléon Architecte* (Paris, 1942); and Edouard Driault, 'Les Monuments d'Austerlitz à Paris', *Revue des Etudes Napoléoniennes*, Vol 41 (1935), pp 129–61.

20 Edward Mogg, *Mogg's New Picture of London; or, Stranger's Guide to the British Metropolis, etc.*, 7th edn (London, 1845).

21 Paris's Pont d'Austerlitz (the first French bridge entirely made of metal) was actually built before 1805 and originally called the Pont du Jardin des Plantes.

22 *La Révolution et l'Empire vus par les historiens du XIXème siècle*, CD-ROM (Cambridge).

23 See Thierry Lentz, 'Le Retour des Cendres', in Bernard Chevallier, Michel Dancoisne-Martineau and Thierry Lentz (eds), *Sainte-Hélène: Ile de Mémoire*, (Paris, 2005), pp 197–213.

24 Jean-Marcel Humbert (ed), *Napoléon aux Invalides: 1840, le Retour des Cendres, Thonon-les-Bains: l'Albaron* (Paris, 1990) p 98.

25 Paris city's symbol is a ship and its motto reads 'Fluctuat nec mergitur, 'it gets tossed about, but it doesn't sink', all too redolent of Trafalgar.

26 Alombert and Colin, *La Campagne de 1805 en Allemagne*.

27 Ronald J Caldwell, *The Era of Napoleon: A Bibliography of the History of Western Civilization, 1799–1815* (New York, 1991).

28 Jean-Marc Largeaud, *Napoléon et Waterloo: la Défaite Glorieuse de 1815 à nos Jours* (Paris, 2006).

29 See also Peter Hicks, 'The Battle of Austerlitz, Collective Anmnesia, and the Non-Commemoration of Napoleon in France', in Holger Hoock (ed), *History, Commemoration, and National Preoccupation: Trafalgar 1805–2005* (Oxford, 2007), pp 119–25.

Index

Alava, Admiral Ignacio, 7, 26, 47, 59
Amiens, Peace of (1802), 71, 80, 87, 90,
    91, 95, 96, 102
Augereau, Marshal Pierre-F-C, 97
Austerlitz, Battle of (1805), 3, 65, 86,
    90, 92, 99, 100, 101, 104–11
Austria, 3, 70, 99, 101–6, 110
Armée, Grande, 3, 30, 70, 86, 90, 91,
    93, 94, 96–100, 107, 110

Barham, see Middleton
Bayntun, Captain Henry, 32, 35
Bernadotte, Marshal, Jean-B-J, 97,
Boulogne, 3, 47, 49, 70, 81, 87, 91, 92,
    96, 97, 99, 100, 102, 104, 105,
    109
Bridge Report (1913), 6, 8, 9, 15, 63
Bruix, Vice Admiral Eustache, 46, 47,
    71

Cádiz, 7, 16, 26, 27, 30, 33, 35, 38, 54,
    59, 61, 66, 67, 70–3, 75, 77, 78
Calder, Vice Admiral Sir Robert, 31, 48,
    49, 59
Canal, Royal Military, 87, 88
Cardinaux, Battle of (1759), 73
Churruca, Captain Cosme, 26, 28, 47,
    49
Codrington, Captain Edward, 11, 21,
    25, 28, 32, 33, 39, 63
Collingwood, Vice Admiral Cuthbert,
    7, 8, 10–12, 15, 16, 28, 30, 31,
    34, 36, 40, 51, 55, 56, 59, 61–5,
    67, 68, 73, 76, 78
Combined Fleet, 5–9, 11–16, 18, 20,
    23–5, 27, 28, 30, 34, 36, 39,
    41–56, 60, 61, 64–6, 70–7, 79
Conn, Captain John, 32
Cooke, Captain John, 32

Copenhagen, Battle of (1801), 2, 5, 8,
    14, 31, 38, 39, 69
Cornwallis, Admiral Sir William, 3, 59
Cosmao-Kerjultan, Captain Julian, 12,
    27, 28, 46, 48, 56

Decrés, Denis, 35, 44, 46, 47, 59, 71
Davout, Marshal Louis, 97–9
Digby, Captain Henry, 13
Duff, Captain George, 19, 33
Dumanoir, Rear Admiral Pierre, 7, 20,
    24, 26, 27, 39, 44, 46, 77
Duncan , Admiral Adam, 44
Dundas, Henry, Viscount Melville,
    30, 31

Escaño, Rear Admiral Antonio, 43, 44,
    47–50, 52–4, 56–9, 68, 74

First of June, Battle of (1794), 60, 73
Fremantle, Captain Thomas, 32, 33,
    39, 65

Ganteaume, Vice Admiral Honoré, 46
Gravina, Admiral Federico, 3, 24, 27,
    28, 35, 44, 46, 47–50, 53, 54,
    60, 71, 74, 78
Grandallana, Domingo, 48
Gibraltar, 6, 14, 43, 46, 49, 51, 56, 66,
    67, 75, 78
Godoy, Manuel, 44

Hamilton, Emma, 35, 38
Hardy, Captain Thomas, 16, 18, 24,
    26, 31, 26
Hewson, Lt George, 38, 40
Howe, Admiral Lord Richard, 44, 73

Keats, Captain Richard, 14, 27, 35, 36

Laforey, Captain Francis, 31, 63
Lannes, Marshal Jean, 97
Latouche-Tréville, Vice Admiral Louis, 47, 71
Lucas, Captain Jean, 20, 46, 52, 64, 76
Louis, Rear Admiral Sir Thomas, 14

Magon, Vice Admiral Charles, 46, 49
Marengo, Battle of (1801), 90, 104, 110
Marmont, Marshal Auguste-F-L, 96, 97
Mazarredo, Admiral José, 42, 45–8
Melville, Viscount, see Dundas
Middleton, Admiral Charles, Lord Barham, 30
Militia, British, 3, 81–3, 85, 87–9

Napoleon I , Emperor of France, 3, 30, 42, 43, 45–7, 57, 59, 60, 66, 67, 70, 71, 79, 81, 82, 87, 89–111
Napoleon III, Emperor of France, 109, 110
Nelson, Vice Admiral Horatio Lord, 1, 2, 6, 8, 10, 12–16, 18, 24, 26–8, 30–41, 43–5, 47, 51, 56, 58–66, 68–70, 73, 75, 76, 78, 79, 87, 90, 100, 101, 111
Ney, Marshal Michel, 97, 98
Nile, Battle of (1798), 2, 5, 7, 8, 14, 31, 32, 36, 38, 39, 60, 61

Pitt, William, 30, 44, 100, 102, 106
Popham, Admiral Sir Home (Telegraphic System), 38

Quiberon Bay, Battle of (1759), 60, 73

Richmond, Duke of, 88
Rodney, Admiral Lord George Brydges, 13, 44, 73
Royal Navy, 2, 6, 8, 10, 30, 41–5, 65, 79, 81, 82, 91, 100
Russia, 95, 99, 101–4, 106
Rutherford, Captain William, 31, 61

St Vincent, Cape, 48, 60, 61
St Vincent, Earl, 61

Ships (British)
Achilles, 22, 26, 31
Africa, 6, 10, 13, 15, 21, 24, 25, 26, 64
Agamemnon, 10, 21, 24, 32
Ajax, 18, 21, 24, 74
Belleisle, 9, 10, 12, 18–24, 63, 74
Bellerophon, 9, 12, 18, 20, 23, 29, 32, 35, 58
Britannia, 13, 14, 18, 21, 24, 26, 58
Colossus, 12, 18, 21, 23
Conqueror, 13, 18, 21, 24, 25, 32, 63–5
Defence, 10, 12, 22, 26
Defiance, 10, 12, 20, 23, 24, 26, 29
Dreadnought, 10, 12, 13, 20, 22–4, 26, 32, 38
Euryalus, 21, 39, 65
Leviathan, 13, 18, 21, 24, 25, 32, 35, 63–5, 74
Minotaur, 20, 24, 26, 63, 74
Neptune, 13, 15, 16, 18, 21, 32, 37, 39, 64, 65
Mars, 10, 12, 19, 21, 22, 33
Orion, 11, 14, 20, 21, 23–6, 32, 39, 63
Polyphemus, 12, 20, 22
Prince, 13, 20, 22, 26
Revenge, 10, 12, 20, 22, 26, 63, 64
Royal Sovereign, 6, 10–13, 16–19, 21, 26, 51, 64, 68, 76
Spartiate, 20, 24, 26, 63, 74
Swiftsure, 12, 20–4, 29, 61
Temeraire, 13, 15, 16, 18, 29, 37, 63, 64, 76
Tonnant, 12, 20, 26, 31, 32, 63, 74
Victory, 6, 12–19, 24, 26, 28, 30–2, 37, 39, 53, 58, 64, 69, 76
Ships (French)
Achille, 12, 20, 22, 26
Aigle, 12, 20, 23, 24, 26, 29, 35, 53
Algésiras, 12, 20, 43, 55
Berwick, 12, 20, 26, 35, 53, 75
Bucentaure, 6–8, 14–18, 22, 24, 32, 39, 53, 63–5, 71, 76, 77
Duguay Trouin, 24, 65

Formidable, 7, 8, 23, 26, 76, 84
Fougueux, 11, 12, 19
Héros, 15, 26, 53, 55
Indomptable, 11, 12, 19, 55, 56
Intrépide, 24–6, 35, 64, 75, 77
Mont Blanc, 24
Neptune, 11, 15, 17, 18, 22–4, 26, 53–5
Pluton, 12, 19, 20, 22–4, 26, 35, 48, 52, 53, 55, 77
Redoutable, 16–21, 24, 52, 53, 64, 76
Scipion, 14, 16, 24
Swiftsure, 12, 21, 75
Ships (Spanish)
    Argonauta, 12, 48, 53, 73
    Bahama, 12, 52, 53
    Firme, 48
    Montañés, 53–6
    Neptuno, 26, 43, 53, 55, 56, 77
    Principé de Asturias, 7, 12, 20, 23, 24, 26, 29, 52–6, 77
    Rayo, 26, 53–6, 73
    San Agustín, 14, 24
    San Francisco de Asís, 26, 53–6
    San Ildefonso, 12, 26
    San Juan Nepomuceno, 9, 16, 20, 26, 52

San Justo, 11, 17, 18, 56
San Leandro, 11, 17, 18, 55
San Rafael, 48
Santa Ana, 7, 11, 18, 19, 21, 22, 42, 43, 52, 53, 55, 73, 77
Santsíma Trinidad, 14, 16, 18, 21, 24–6, 52–6, 63–5, 76, 77
Strachan, Captain Sir Richard, 65, 66
Soult, Marshal Nicholas-J, 97, 98

Trafalgar, Battle of (1805) , 1–6, 8, 10, 13–15, 18, 19, 26–8, 30, 31, 34, 36, 37, 41–7, 51, 54–6, 58–61, 64–71, 73, 74, 77–9, 89–91, 99–101, 104, 107, 111
Tyler, Captain Charles, 31, 32

Ulm, Capitulation of (1805), 86, 101, 105, 107

Villeneuve, Vice Admiral Pierre, 3, 6, 7, 14, 16, 20, 23, 26, 28, 35, 37, 42, 44–51, 53, 59, 60, 66, 70–2, 74, 75, 77, 78, 105
Volunteer movement, 3, 68, 81, 83–7, 89, 98
West Indies, 36, 37, 59